Reading Comprehension Test Papers

Test Papers

GEOFFREY LAND

Oxford University Press

Oxford University Press, Walton Street, Oxford OX2 6DP

Oxford London
New York Toronto Melbourne Auckland
Petaling Jaya Singapore Hong Kong Tokyo
Delhi Bombay Calcutta Madras Karachi
Nairobi Dar es Salaam Cape Town

and associated companies in
Berlin Ibadan

OXFORD, OXFORD ENGLISH, and the OXFORD ENGLISH
logo are trade marks of Oxford University Press

ISBN 0 19 432785 X

© Oxford University Press 1975

First published 1975
Eighth impression 1990

Phototypeset by Tradespools Ltd, Frome, Somerset
Printed in Hong Kong

Contents

Acknowledgements

The publisher and author wish to thank the following for their permission to use extracts from copyright material:

The Estate of W. Somerset Maugham and William Heinemann Ltd. (p. 11, from 'The Happy Man' from the *Complete Short Stories of W. Somerset Maugham*; p. 125, from *Cakes and Ale* by W. Somerset Maugham); Rupert Hart-Davis (p. 21, from *Menagerie Manor* by Gerald Durrell); Coronet Press Ltd. (p. 24, from *Cat's Prey* by Dorothy Eden); Methuen & Co. Ltd. (p. 31, from *The World in the Evening* by Christopher Isherwood); Victor Gollancz Ltd. (p. 34, from *Adrift in Soho* by Colin Wilson; p. 65, from *Gaudy Night* by Dorothy L. Sayers; p. 105, from *Flight of the Falcon* by Daphne du Maurier); Michael Joseph Ltd. (p. 42, from *One Pair of Hands* by Monica Dickens; p. 56, from *Doctor in the House* by Richard Gordon); Hutchinson Publishing Group Ltd. (p. 45, from *Good Evening, Everyone* by A. J. Alan); Michael Joseph Ltd. and Penguin Books Ltd. (p. 63, from 'The Landlady' from *Kiss, Kiss* by Roald Dahl); Hodder and Stoughton Limited (p. 73, from *A Terrace in the Sun* by Cecil Roberts); William Collins & Co. Ltd. (p. 87, from *The Curse of the Kings* by Victoria Holt); Macmillan and St. Martin's Press, Inc. (p. 95, from *The Last Enemy* by Richard Hillary); William Heinemann Ltd. and Curtis Brown Ltd. (p. 115, from *The Nightcomers* by Eric Ambler); the Author (p. 128, from *Image of Love* by William E. Barret).

Introduction

To the Teacher

These test papers have been compiled to provide practice material for students preparing for the Cambridge First Certificate in English. Though teachers will, I hope, find the material interesting, and may like to use some of the exercises in class as the basis of a lesson, students intending to sit this examination should be accustomed from the very outset of their course to working within the time limit. Each year many failures are attributed not so much to lack of knowledge as to students' plodding through the examinations papers far too slowly. When the allotted time is up, they have very often done little more than half the paper; even if this half were perfect, it would not be sufficient for the student to pass. Bearing this in mind, teachers must insist that the time limit is strictly adhered to every time one of these papers is set as a class exercise. For this reason, and by the very nature of the questions, the test papers are not suitable for use as homework.

To the Student

The time allowed for the Reading Comprehension Paper of the Cambridge First Certificate examination is 1¼ hours. This means that you must spend *no more than half an hour* (and probably less) on Section A, and half an hour on Section B. This will allow you at least fifteen minutes for reading through what you have written and making any alterations you may find necessary.

Section A. Read the instructions carefully. You are asked to choose the word or phrase which *best* completes each sentence. In most cases, only one of the five words or phrases given is possible. In the event of there being more than one possibility, you must choose the word that makes the finished sentence logical and sensible. You should be able to complete this section fairly quickly. Do not be put off if you are not familiar with all five words or phrases printed under the sentence. You will probably be able to recognize the correct one nevertheless. *Work fast!* And do not waste time thinking about any question you do not understand. As this is a test of vocabulary – in other words, to find out which words you know – no amount of reflection will lead you to understand words you have never seen before. If you don't know the answer immediately, the only thing you can do is to make a quick guess and then go on to the next question. Remember, you are working against time, and you only have thirty minutes at the most to deal with forty sentences.

Section B. There are two passages to read here, each one followed by ten multiple-choice questions. Spend no more than fifteen minutes on each passage and its questions. Remember this, as it is important – it is far better to leave one set of questions unfinished and go on to the next one rather than to finish the first perfectly and then have no time to start the second.

Read each passage through carefully before looking at the questions that follow it. If you have understood the passage well, the multiple choice questions should not give you much difficulty. Only one of the four suggested answers will agree *exactly* with the facts you have read in the passage, although the others may form quite good sentences.

At the end of an hour you will have finished the paper. Use the last fifteen minutes to read it over again, to fill in any blanks that you have left, and to change any answer if you have had second thoughts – but be careful! Second thoughts are not *always* better.

Test Paper 1

Section A

*In this section you must choose the word or phrase which best
completes each sentence. Cross through the letter A, B, C, D or E
for the word or phrase you choose. Give one answer only to each
question.*

1   It was .... with rain, and we got wet through.
    A showering   B trickling   C pouring   D falling
    E rushing

2   She rushed out of the room in a very bad temper, ... the
    door behind her.
    A slapping   B beating   C crashing   D slamming
    E smacking

3   Our letters are .... every morning at eight o'clock.
    A delivered   B restored   C allowed   D delayed
    E arrived

4   He pretended to be brave, but he was really a ...., afraid
    of everything.
    A timid   B coward   C fear   D mouse   E quaker

5   Mary fell .... with her fiancé over the question of where
    they were to be married.
    A over   B through   C out   D down   E about

6   The wedding was to have been in May, but now it has
    been .... until July.
    A postponed   B cancelled   C delayed   D altered
    E changed

7   My wife was very .... when I laughed at her new hair-do.
    A happy   B anxious   C upset   D ashamed   E desperate

8. I was very ashamed when I .... that I had made such a silly mistake.
A recognized   B learned   C hoped   D thought
E realized

9. Be careful how you go. It is freezing and the roads are
....
A slippery   B smooth   C iced   D covered   E muddy

10. It's raining hard now. Let's stand in that doorway to ....
A protect   B dry   C save   D prevent   E shelter

11. I heard the clock .... eleven, so I knew I was not too late.
A ring   B make   C strike   D say   E sound

12. My watch had run .... so I didn't know what the time
was.
A out   B up   C in   D through   E down

13. I wish that noise would stop. It gets on my ....
A head   B brain   C feelings   D nerves   E hair

14. It is such a stupid film that it would be .... of time and
money to go and see it.
A a loss   B a drop   C a waste   D an expense   E a fall

15. The actors were pleased that there was such a large ....
for the first night of the new play.
A congregation   B assembly   C congress   D meeting
E audience

16. It was a very cold night, and we stood .... at the bus-
stop, waiting for the last bus.
A shivering   B trembling   C quivering   D shaking
E vibrating

17. I can't .... £5 for one book! Haven't you got a cheaper
edition?
A provide   B dispose   C allow   D afford   E cost

18. What .... is your father's new car?
A mark   B make   C brand   D kind   E sort

19 I'm afraid we shall have to call .... the match on account of the bad weather.
A on B in C out D off E back

20 Uncle Sebastian left me £3,000 in his ....
A inheritance B testament C will D wishes E estate

21 My brother is really too kind: everybody takes .... of him.
A profit B advantage C cost D example E occasion

22 This light is too .... for me to read by. Haven't we got a stronger bulb somewhere?
A dark B little C slight D weak E dim

23 I'm afraid I'm rather .... of hearing. Will you speak a little louder, please?
A stiff B hard C slow D quiet E deaf

24 We'd better .... the garden this evening. It hasn't rained for over two weeks.
A damp B wet C moisten D water E soak

25 Just put the dirty dishes in the .... We'll wash them up later on.
A bath B wash-basin C tub D sink E bucket

26 There is no spoon in my saucer. Will you lend me yours to .... my coffee with?
A stir B mix C agitate D disturb E beat

27 It took her several weeks to .... from the shock.
A restore B recover C survive D get over E improve

28 I can't .... that noise any longer! Either you sell that trumpet or you leave this house.
A hold B support C like D want E stand

29 Her face is not very attractive, but she has a marvellous ....
A form B figure C shape D curve E line

30 My three daughters would like to have dancing lessons, but the .... are very expensive.
A prices   B costs   C wages   D salaries   E fees

31 When I went to the doctor, he told me I must give .... smoking.
A in   B over   C up   D back   E out

32 The cathedral was very carefully .... last century.
A mended   B built   C restored   D replaced   E redone

33 'What a pretty baby, Mrs Jones! I can see that he takes .... you!'
A after   B over   C like   D from   E by

34 While the children were playing on the beach, Molly .... on a broken bottle and cut her foot rather badly.
A ran   B trod   C walked   D tripped   E came

35 You should have taken the butter out of the refrigerator; it is too hard to .... on the bread.
A smear   B lie   C rub   D spread   E cut

36 They .... at the notice but the light was too dim for them to read it.
A looked   B peeped   C glared   D peered   E eyed

37 'Get out of my garden, you horrible little boys!' the man shouted, shaking his .... at the children.
A hand   B leg   C head   D fist   E hair

38 I was so tired when I got home last night that I fell asleep the moment my head touched the ....
A door-bell   B pillow   C cushion   D blanket   E bed

39 'How much bread do you want, Barry?' 'Two .... please, Mother.'
A slices   B layers   C flakes   D lumps   E crumbs

40 We will get married as soon as we have .... the problem of where we are going to live.
A resolved   B achieved   C managed   D answered   E settled

10

Section B

In this section you will find after each of the passages a number of questions or unfinished statements about the passage, each with four suggested ways of finishing it. You must choose the one which you think fits best. Cross through the letter A, B, C or D for the answer you choose. Give one answer only to each question. Read each passage right through before choosing your answers.

First Passage

Late one afternoon, when I was beginning to think that I had worked enough for that day, I heard a ring at the bell. I opened the door to a total stranger. He asked me my name; I told him. He asked if he might come in.

'Certainly.'   5

I led him into my sitting-room and begged him to sit down. He seemed a trifle embarrassed. I offered him a cigarette and he had some difficulty in lighting it without letting go of his hat. When he had satisfactorily achieved this feat I asked him if I should not put it on a chair for him. He quickly did this and   10
while doing it dropped his umbrella.

'I hope you don't mind my coming to see you like this,' he said. 'My name is Stephens and I am a doctor. You're in the medical, I believe?'

'Yes, but I don't practise.'   15

'No, I know. I've just read a book of yours about Spain and I wanted to ask you about it.'

'It's not a very good book, I'm afraid.'

'The fact remains that you know something about Spain and there's no one else I know who does. And I thought perhaps you   20
wouldn't mind giving me some information.'

'I shall be very glad.'

He was silent for a moment. He reached out for his hat and holding it in one hand absent-mindedly stroked it with the other. I imagined that it gave him confidence.   25

'I hope you won't think it very odd for a perfect stranger to talk to you like this.' He gave an apologetic laugh. 'I'm not going to tell you the story of my life.'

When people say this to me I always know that it is precisely what they are going to do. I do not mind. In fact, I rather like it.   30

'I was brought up by two old aunts. I've never been anywhere.

11

I've never done anything. I've been married for six years. I have no children. I'm a medical officer at the Camberwell Infirmary. I can't stick it any more.'

41 When the man rang the writer's bell, the writer
    A   had stopped work.
    B   was thinking of stopping work.
    C   was opening the door.
    D   would have liked to stop work.

42 The writer was surprised when he opened the door because
    A   the man was a foreigner.
    B   the man knew his name.
    C   the man had rung the bell.
    D   he had never seen the man before.

43 How did the visitor behave in the writer's sitting-room?
    A   He moved quickly.
    B   He kept his hat on.
    C   He did not sit down.
    D   He was nervous.

44 Of the two people in the story
    A   one was a doctor and the other was not.
    B   they were both practising doctors.
    C   they were both qualified doctors.
    D   they were both writers.

45 Stephens had come to visit the writer because
    A   he wanted to give him some information.
    B   he wanted him to give him some information.
    C   he wanted some information about him.
    D   he wanted to inform him about something.

46 Why had Stephens come to see this particular man?
    A   Because Stephens knew a lot about Spain.
    B   Because he wanted to tell the writer the story of his life.
    C   Because the writer was the only person who could tell him what he wanted.
    D   Because he was particularly interested in Spanish life and literature.

47 What sort of man was the writer?
   A Shy and nervous
   B Curious
   C Interested in other people
   D Talkative

48 When people say to the writer 'I'm not going to tell you the story of my life'
   A he does not believe them.
   B he gets angry.
   C he can't do anything about it.
   D he tries to stop them.

49 Stephens was
   A happily married.
   B ambitious, and wanted a better-paid job.
   C fed up with his job.
   D living with two old aunts.

50 Stephens complained that his work was
   A very hard.
   B badly paid.
   C boring.
   D unusual.

Second Passage

My great-aunt Emma was rather a terrifying old lady. She
had been the headmistress of quite an important girls' boarding-
school – run, however, on her own inflexible and old-fashioned
lines – and she had come, over the years, to look upon everyone
as backward and potentially naughty school-girls. This applied   5
particularly to members of her own family. My brother and I
were never very happy when she came to visit us and used to
spend as much time out of the house as we possibly could. And
if Mother wanted us to go to Aunt Emma's for any reason (she
lived in Castleton, which was about twenty-five miles away)   10
we would go to any lengths to find an excuse. Luckily for us,
even though she had given up teaching many years before, she
still led a very full social life and had little time for family
visits.
   But I remember that on one occasion she came to our house   15
for a long week-end during the summer. I think she had had
flu, or something like that; at any rate, Mother had had an

13

attack of conscience about not seeing the old thing for such a
long time and thought that a few days by the sea would do her
good. George and I were sent to the station to meet her, and this
time we hadn't been able to find a reasonable excuse to get out
of it.

There was no doubt about our being able to recognize her as
she was always dressed in the same fashion, summer or winter,
in a tweed suit, a felt hat that looked like a man's, and stout
walking shoes. It was not that she was short of clothes; in fact
she had a vast selection, but they all looked exactly the same.
Mother suggested that perhaps she bought them wholesale.

George and I wondered if she would know us, since we had
not seen her for a year or two. She did, of course, and she greeted
us in her usual fashion.

'Well, George, you've certainly grown since I saw you last.
Stand up straight, boy. Which class are you in now? The
fourth form? Good. You shall show me your books later. And
Peter, you've left school I hear. Why didn't you stay on and try
for the University? What are you doing? In a bank, aren't you?
I'll ask you some questions about that later. Take my case, boy.
And this bag too, please.'

Before we could attempt to reply to any of this, she had swept
us out of the station and had started to shout 'Taxi!' at the top
of her voice, and to wave the heavy masculine-looking walking-
stick that she always carried. Aunt Emma's voice had great
carrying power, and several taxi-drivers, standing by their
cabs on the other side of the station forecourt, jumped guiltily.
One got into his cab and started the engine.

'But, Aunt Emma,' I said, at the same time making a gesture
of refusal at the taxi-driver, who got out of his taxi looking
bewildered and rather annoyed. 'We don't need a taxi. I've got
the car over there.'

'Car!' She sounded surprised. 'Whose car? Who's driving it?'
'My car, and I'm driving it,' I replied.

'Are you sure you know how to drive?' she demanded
suspiciously.

'Of course, Aunt Emma. I've had a licence for nearly two
years.'

'All right, then,' she conceded, unwillingly, 'but go very
slowly. I shall sit in the front with you to make sure that you
do. You go in the back, George, and don't talk. Peter must
concentrate on the driving.'

14

51 At the time of the story Aunt Emma was
    A   ill.
    B   a headmistress.
    (C)   a retired teacher.
    D   a socialist.

52 Aunt Emma used to
    A   think her relations were school-children.
    (B)   treat everyone like school-girls.
    C   consider her family unintelligent.
    D   look backwards at everyone.

53 Aunt Emma and the writer
    A   were not on good terms.
    (B)   seldom saw each other.
    C   visited each other reluctantly.
    D   did not like each other very much.

54 Why did the writer's mother invite Aunt Emma for the
    week-end?
    (A)   She was ashamed that they had not seen each other
          recently.
    B   The old lady came for a week-end every summer.
    C   Aunt Emma wanted to spend a week-end by the sea.
    D   She was a conscientious woman.

55 How was Aunt Emma dressed when she arrived at the
    station?
    A   Suitably for the occasion.
    (B)   The same as always.
    C   Fashionably.
    D   In a most unusual fashion.

56 The writer's mother thought that Aunt Emma bought her
    clothes
    A   at sales.
    (B)   in large quantities.
    C   second-hand.
    D   frequently.

15

57 From Aunt Emma's ~~remarks~~ *talking*, we learn that
   A George and Peter were students.
   B Peter was not clever at school.
   C George was doing well at school.
   D Peter was working.

58 The taxi-drivers
   A were lazy and didn't want to work.
   B thought that Aunt Emma was a police-woman.
   C were startled by Aunt Emma's voice.
   D were all very busy.

59 The taxi-driver got out of his cab because
   A Aunt Emma shouted at him.
   B Aunt Emma and the two boys got into a car.
   C he was a little angry.
   D Peter waved at him.

60 Aunt Emma told George
   A not to drive the car.
   B not to sit in the front.
   C to let Peter drive.
   D not to disturb Peter.

Test Paper 2

Section A

In this section you must choose the word or phrase which best completes each sentence. Cross through the letter A, B, C, D or E for the word or phrase you choose. Give one answer only for each question.

1   Please .... me that I have an important appointment at three o'clock.
    A remember B recall C remind D think
    E call to mind

2   So you are leaving for London tomorrow! I hope you have a good ....
    A trip B travel C going D excursion E route

3   She promised that she would pay me this week, but she didn't .... her word.
    A hold B stay C remember D support E keep

4   I .... your pardon; I had no idea this was your seat.
    A ask B beg C hope D want E need

5   Don't be rude to your father, Paul; you should .... a good example to your little brother.
    A give B show C make D set E keep

6   She is only three and she hasn't learned to .... the time yet.
    A tell B say C know D understand E read

7   There's no need to get so angry; keep your ....
    A calm B mind C face D mood E temper

17

8　If you tell Margaret, everyone will know by tomorrow; she can never .... a secret.
Ⓐ keep　**B** hold　**C** tell　**D** contain　**E** save

9　My boss is very critical, and he is always finding ....
with my work.
A trouble　**B** mistakes　**C** criticism　**D** error　Ⓔ fault

10　The cigarette-end .... fire to the dry grass, and soon the whole forest was alight.
A put　Ⓑ set　**C** gave　**D** made　**E** let

11　You should always .... the plates with clean water after you have washed them.
A soak　**B** splash　**C** wet　**D** damp　Ⓔ rinse

12　Aunt Fanny was .... ill very suddenly in church one Sunday morning.
A made　**B** got　**C** seen　Ⓓ taken　**E** fallen

13　'What does your boy-friend do for a ....?' 'He's a bank clerk.'
Ⓐ living　**B** job　**C** career　**D** post　**E** salary

14　It was an accident, sir! I didn't do it on ....!
A intention　**B** wish　Ⓒ purpose　**D** deliberation
E desire

15　Hurry up! The train leaves in ten minutes. We don't want to .... it.
A waste　**B** lose　**C** drop　Ⓓ miss　**E** lack

16　Barker .... two goals in the last ten minutes, so our club won the match.
A made　**B** shot　Ⓒ scored　**D** passed　**E** marked

17　This is an official enquiry, and you must .... the truth.
A say　Ⓑ tell　**C** speak　**D** show　**E** answer

18　You have a very nasty cough. You must .... on cigarettes.
A put out　**B** give up　**C** reduce　Ⓓ cut down
E take down

18

19　I am working very hard at the moment, because I am going to .... my final examinations next month.
A get　B pass　C receive　(D) take　E give

20　I'm sorry I am so late, sir. My alarm clock didn't ....
A ring　B come on　(C) go off　D sound　E take off

21　I .... with you in your great trouble, and I wish I could help in some way.
(A) sympathize　B agree　C feel　D console　E assist

22　A gang of thieves .... the bank late on Saturday night.
A stole　B took　C broke　D cleaned　(E) robbed

23　The horizon is an imaginary line. It doesn't really ....
A happen　B be　C take place　(D) exist　E seem

24　It was evening when we reached the village, and .... was gathering over the stream.
A fog　B steam　(C) mist　D vapour　E smoke

25　Mr Oakes .... very fine roses in his garden.
A makes　B raises　C breeds　(D) grows　E develops

26　Eloise was .... when she heard that she had not got the job she applied for.
A deluded　B down　C beaten　(D) disappointed
E deceived

27　We shall have to go on to the next village. It's too late to .... now.
A set back　B turn in　C set in　D turn round
(E) turn back

28　Mr Elmes .... at the age of 65 and went to live in a little cottage by the sea.
A retreated　B repelled　C withdrew　D surrendered
(E) retired

29　I went to see Angela in hospital yesterday evening. She is getting better but she is still too .... to talk much.
(A) weak　B fragile　C delicate　D thin　E feeble

19

30 You completely misunderstood my instructions; you got hold of the wrong end of the ....

A string B stick C line D rope E story

31 Old Mrs Bush always keeps a pistol under her pillow because she is very ....

A afraid B worried C shy D nervous E sensitive

32 I ran .... Peter Larch in the street yesterday; we hadn't seen each other for ages.

A over B down C into D in E around

33 Would you mind opening the window just a little? It's terribly .... in here.

A dull B thick C dense D tedious E stuffy

34 Put that orange .... in the waste-paper basket, not on the floor!

A rind B peel C skin D shell E husk

35 'I'm glad to see you looking so well, Mr Hedge.' 'Yes, I feel as .... as a fiddle.'

A well B young C straight D fit E fine

36 Unfortunately Freda is not a very good ...., and instead of hitting the target she shot Miss Pettigrew, who was standing on the other side of the field.

A gunner B shooter C rifleman D shot E striker

37 Uncle Max slipped as he was walking beside the river, and fell into the water with a loud ....

A splash B bang C trickle D thud E crash

38 The *Queen Elizabeth II* .... from Southampton at 10.45 tomorrow.

A parts B sails C steams D leaves E embarks

39 There is a .... going round that Jimmy is going to marry rich old Mrs Twigg. Do you think it is true?

A rumour B noise C whisper D scandal E gossip

40 I only know that it is true that he has broken .... his engagement to Pamela.

A off B with C up D down E out

slave 勞錄.   wood splint 木刺   zoo-keeper 動物管理員
blondlion-nice and stupid
darklion-fierce and clever

Section B

*In this section you will find after each of the passages a number
of questions or unfinished statements about the passage, each
with four suggested ways of finishing it. You must choose the
one which you think fits best. Cross through the letter A, B, C
or D for the answer you choose. Give one answer only to each
question. Read each passage right through before choosing your
answers.* Leo was a new born lion. He grew so quick
and came so big that

First Passage
*In this passage Gerald Durrell is describing the arrival of a lion
at his Zoo in Jersey.* Leo is a young lion. He moved to a new cage, which was

Another newcomer was our lion, who went under the time-
honoured name of Leo. He was one of the famous Dublin Zoo
lions and was probably about the fiftieth generation born in
captivity. On his arrival he was only about the size of a small
dog, and so he was housed in a cage in the Mammal House, but   5
he grew at such a pace that it was soon imperative that we find
him more spacious quarters. We had just finished construction *building*
on a large cage for the chimpanzees, and decided we would
put Leo in that until we could get around to building him a
cage of his own.   10
So Leo was transferred, and settled down very happily. I was
glad to see, when his mane started to develop, that he was going
to be a blond lion, for in my experience the lions with blond
manes, as opposed to dark manes, have always nice, if slightly *a little*
stupid characters.   15
This theory has been borne out by Leo's behaviour. He had in
his cage a large log as a plaything and a big, black rubber
bucket in which he received his water ration. This bucket
fascinated him, and after he had drunk his fill he would upset
the remains of the water and then pat the bucket with his great   20
paws, making it roll round the cage so that he could stalk it
and pounce on it. *playful*
One day I was in the grounds when a lady stopped me to
inquire whether we had acquired Leo from a circus. Slightly
puzzled, I said 'No,' and asked her why she should think so.   25
'Because,' she replied, 'he was doing such clever tricks.' I
discovered that he had, by some extraordinary means, managed
to wedge the rubber bucket on his head, and was walking round
and round the cage proudly, wearing it like a hat.

mischievous 惡作劇〉

21

when leo was one year ago he started to roar at first
He did not have to much confidence to do that
so he

30   In his second year, Leo decided, after mature reflection, that
it was a lion's duty to roar. He was not awfully sure how to go
about it, so he would retire to quiet corners of his cage and
practise very softly to himself, for he was rather shy of this
new accomplishment and would stop immediately and pretend
35 it was nothing to do with him if you came in view.

When he was satisfied that the sound was right and his breath
control perfect, he treated us to his first concert. It was a
wonderful moonlight night when he started, and we were all
delighted that Leo was, at last, a proper lion. A lion roaring
40 sounds just like someone sawing wood on a gigantic, echoing
barrel. The first coughs or rasps are quick and fairly close
together, and you can imagine the saw biting into the wood;
then the coughs slow down and become more drawn out, and
suddenly stop, and you instinctively wait to hear the thud of
45 the sawn-off piece hitting the ground.

The trouble was that Leo was so proud of his accomplishment
that he could not wait until nightfall to give us the benefit of
his vocal cords. He started roaring earlier and earlier each
evening, and would keep it up solidly all night, with five-
50 minute intervals for meditation in between each roar. Sometimes, when he was in particularly good voice, you could
imagine that he was sitting on the end of your bed, serenading
you. We found that if we opened the bedroom window and
shouted 'Leo, shut up!' this had the effect of silencing him for
55 half an hour; but at the end of that time he would decide that
you had not really meant it and would start all over again.

(margin notes: rough and dull; sounding; sawdust; troublesome)

41 The family of lions that Leo came from
    A   lived in a zoo in Dublin.
    B   had lived in zoos for very many years.
    C   were very small.
    D   was a large family of about fifty lions.

42 Why was it necessary to build Leo another cage?
    A   Because the cage he was in was needed for the chim-
         panzees.
    B   Because he didn't like being in the Mammal House.
    C   Because he had got too big for the old cage.
    D   Because the old cage wasn't strong enough to hold
         him.

Leo first concert took place at night his roaring was rough and
dull just like the sawing of wood
Afterward Leo roar continuously with only few minutes intervals
in between each roar. People became tired of his roaring.

lions → roar   cats → purr, mew
dogs → bark   pigs → grunt

43 The writer thinks that blond lions
    A are pleasant and rather silly.
    B have good characters.
    C are better than lions with dark manes.
    D have very little brain.

44 The writer's opinion of blond lions
    A has been changed by Leo's behaviour.
    B has been verified by Leo's intelligence.
    C has been proved wrong.
    D is still the same as it was before.

45 Why did Leo have a bucket in his cage?
    A To play with.
    B To drink from.
    C To put on his head.
    D To roll round the cage.

46 The lady asked if Leo had been in a circus because
    A he had a bucket on his head.
    B she had taught him some tricks.
    C he had tricked her.
    D the writer was puzzled.

47 Leo started to roar when he was
    A one year old.
    B mature.
    C two years old.
    D shy.

48 Before Leo roared for his 'first concert'
    A he went into a corner of the cage.
    B he made sure he could do it properly.
    C all the people at the zoo were delighted.
    D he became rather shy.

49 Why were the people at the zoo rather sorry later on that
    Leo had started roaring?
    A Because he stopped every five minutes.
    B He roared at night with five minute intervals.
    C He kept them awake.
    D He used to sit on the end of their beds.

23

50 Shouting at Leo
   A had no effect at all.
   B kept him quiet for a little.
   C made him stop roaring.
   D was not meant seriously.

Second Passage

Mrs Henrietta Conroy looks out of her bedroom window and sees lights in a nearby house, The Hilltop, which she knows to be empty.

'Dougal!' Her penetrating voice had come excitedly down the stairs. 'Come quickly! I think there must be burglars at The Hilltop.'

5 Dougal didn't shout from the bottom of the stairs because he knew it was useless. His mother was slightly deaf. He came up to the picturesque, untidy room with its embarrassing collection of photographs of himself at various sizes, its comfortable chairs (his mother was a large woman and liked comfort), its book-lined walls that held every type of book from Hans

10 Andersen to *The Decameron*, and its superb view of the hill that leaned its golden bosom against the apple green sunset sky.

All the long windows of the old white two-winged house on the crest of the hill were lighted.

'No, Mother,' said Dougal, 'what burglars would be stupid

15 enough to put all the lights on?'

'Then who is it up there?' Henrietta demanded. 'Should we notify the police?'

'The new owners would hardly appreciate that.'

'Who?'

20 'The new owners,' Dougal shouted.

Henrietta looked at him with her prominent indignant eyes. It seemed to Dougal that indignation was their most frequent expression and that he was the reason for it.

'Dougal, you didn't tell me that The Hilltop was sold.'

25 'The sale was only finalized last week, Mother.'

'Last week! Seven whole days ago. You make me live in ignorance of what is going on under my very nose.'

Dougal moved his hands resignedly. It was useless to point out to Henrietta that the first essential when one followed the

30 profession of law was discretion. His father, in thirty years, had not been able to convince her of that, so how could he, who

24

[handwritten: she always wanted to know everything.]
[handwritten: Both the fanther and son are lawyer.]

she had always expected to come to her with everything?

His mother was an incurable gossip and, like all gossips, she liked to be the first among her friends with new titbits. She found it humiliating to hear from others what her own son had 35 known, professionally, for some time.

But he admitted that he could have told her The Hilltop was sold. There would have been no harm in that.

'I'm sorry, Mother. The transaction wasn't completed until today. The Mildmays are moving in at once. Or rather Simon 40 Mildmay's fiancée is. They're being married in a few days.'

Henrietta sat down, spreading out her wide lap. Her broad, *[handwritten: wide]* *[handwritten: simple]* plain, highly-coloured face was full of charm and kindness.

'A wedding! How exciting! Now, Dougal, be sweet and tell me all about these people.' *[handwritten: She was pleased with the good]* 45 *[handwritten: news that there was going to have a wedding]*

51 Dougal went upstairs to his mother's room
  (A) to talk to her.
  B to look out of the window at The Hilltop.
  C to see if there were burglars at The Hilltop.
  D to look at the sunset.

52 Why didn't Dougal shout from downstairs?
  A Because he wanted to talk to his mother privately.
  (B) Because his mother wouldn't have heard.
  C Because his mother wasn't listening.
  D Because his mother was looking out of the window.

53 What did Dougal know that his mother didn't know?
  A That there were burglars at The Hilltop.
  B That burglars were not usually stupid.
  C That the police had been notified.
  (D) That The Hilltop had been sold.

54 Henrietta asks 'Who?' (line 19) because
  A she did not hear what her son said.
  (B) she was so surprised that she could not believe her ears.
  C she wanted to know who the new owners were.
  D she wanted to know who was in The Hilltop.

55 Dougal thought that
  A Henrietta often looked prominent.
  (B) he often made his mother look indignant.

C his mother's expression was most prominent in her eyes.

D Henrietta's prominent eyes were frequently expressive.

56 What do you know about Dougal's profession?

   A He was a professional man, but we don't know exactly what.

   B He was an estate agent and had organized the sale of The Hilltop.

   C He was a lawyer, like his father.

   D We know nothing at all about his profession.

57 Henrietta Conroy was a woman who

   A talked too much.

   B liked to know everything about her neighbours.

   C was never convinced of anything.

   D was often humiliated by other people.

58 Very often, Dougal Conroy did not give his mother pieces of information because

   A he was not interested in gossip.

   B he had no information that would have interested her.

   C he had to keep quiet for professional reasons.

   D he did not want to encourage his mother to gossip.

59 The Hilltop was to be occupied at once by

   A Mr and Mrs Mildmay.

   B Mr Mildmay, and Mrs Mildmay later.

   C Mrs Mildmay, and Mr Mildmay later.

   D a woman.

60 Henrietta stopped being indignant with Dougal when

   A she learned that there was going to be a wedding.

   B Dougal told her that the Mildmays were moving to The Hilltop.

   C she heard that Simon Mildmay was engaged.

   D Dougal told her that The Hilltop was sold.

Test Paper 3

Section A

In this section you must choose the word or phrase which best completes each sentence. Cross through the letter A, B, C, D or E for the word or phrase you choose. Give one answer only for each question.

1   She .... the tablecloth carefully and put it away in a drawer.
    A divided   **B** pleated   **C** bent   **D** creased   **E** folded

2   'Let's go for a walk in the park.' 'Yes, that is a good ....'
    A idea   **B** think   **C** discovery   **D** opinion
    E programme

3   A strong wind was blowing, and all the windows of the old house were ....
    A trembling   **B** shivering   **C** banging   **D** hammering
    E rattling

4   You shouldn't leave your bicycle outside in the rain. It will get ....
    A muddy   **B** oxydized   **C** rusty   **D** broken   **E** torn

5   I would be very .... if you could give me Mrs Arbuthnot's address.
    A grateful   **B** gratified   **C** pleasant   **D** contented
    E satisfied

6   I shall have to get .... to have a look at my car. It isn't working properly.
    A an engineer   **B** a technician   **C** a mechanic
    D a blacksmith   **E** an ironmonger

27

7   'What a beautiful pearl necklace!' 'The pearls are not
    ...., I'm afraid.'
    A true B right C good D actual E real

8   Don't .... me! It wasn't my fault!
    A criticize B blame C convict D condemn
    E indicate

9   My brother's .... is stamp-collecting.
    A sport B occupation C wish D job E hobby

10 When he was eighteen, Tom Laurel decided to .... the
    army.
    A join B reach C become D member E belong

11 The doctor advised Aunt Penelope to take a .... rest
    for a month.
    A total B absolute C whole D complete E full

12 That was a delicious meal! Would you give me the ....,
    please? I would like to cook it for my husband.
    A formula B recipe C prescription D instructions
    E rules

13 Barbiturates are drugs which are often used in the ....
    of emotional disorders.
    A cure B recovery C improvement D healing
    E treatment

14 You are getting too old for football, Mr Bracken. You'd
    better take .... golf instead.
    A on B in C off D up E over

15 Would you mind .... the light on? It's getting very dark
    in here.
    A setting B getting C putting D letting E taking

16 I have .... out of sugar, so I must go to the grocer's and
    get some.
    A come B run C gone D worked E used

28

17 You shouldn't walk around with .... feet, Freddy. The floor isn't very clean.
A nude B naked C bare D uncovered E stripped

18 Who gave you .... to leave your car there, in front of the Royal Palace?
A possibility B liberty C law D permission E licence

19 Was my name .... during the conversation?
A told B said C pronounced D mentioned E talked

20 Would you .... the salt, please?
A give B let C pass D deliver E carry

21 I would love to go to the exhibition with you, but I'm afraid I can't .... the time.
A spare B lose C waste D leave E save

22 That's a very .... suit you are wearing. Is it a new one?
A tasty B proper C well-dressed D polite E smart

23 We have had to raise our prices because of the increase in the cost of .... materials.
A raw B crude C natural D unworked E original

24 The weather forecast promises a sunny morning, but there may be a .... or two in the afternoon.
A rain B drop C fall D bad weather E shower

25 I was .... asleep when you arrived; that's why I didn't hear you knock at first.
A quite B fast C totally D dead E all

26 Can you tell me the .... to the station, please?
A road B way C route D direction E street

27 Cousin Belinda is very ...., and blushes whenever a boy speaks to her.
A nervous B doubtful C frightened D worried E shy

29

28 Go straight down this road and take the second .... on the left.
A point   B corner   C angle   D place   (E) turning

29 We .... to inform you that your account is three months overdue.
A apologize   (B) regret   C are unwilling   D dislike
E are displeased

30 I want to .... you on your engagement.
A compliment   B praise   C wish   D welcome
(E) congratulate

31 The doorway was very dark, and I .... at the names printed under the bells, trying to read them.
A watched   B glanced   (C) peered   D peeped   E looked

32 Aunt Bertha is trying to .... her husband to buy her a fur coat.
(A) persuade   B tell   C influence   D talk   E make

33 Our visit to the south of France was put off .... to my wife's illness.
(A) owing   B because   C resulting   D reasonable
E on account

34 I try to put .... a little money each week towards my summer holidays.
A back   (B) by   C off   D on   E down

35 The signature on that old painting is so .... that I can hardly read it.
A low   B unclear   C weak   (D) faint   E dim

36 A sudden loud noise behind me nearly made me jump out of my ....
A self   B clothes   C shoes   (D) skin   E nerves

37 The next .... on the programme will be a song by Harry and Laura.
A piece   B bit   C unit   D part   (E) item

38 I am very .... to know the result of the test. Please tell me, doctor.
A worried B anxious C disturbed D alarmed
E uneasy

39 There is a lot of water on the floor. I think the washing-machine must be ....
A losing B leaking C dripping D running
E dropping

40 Baby has put a button in his mouth. Quick! Take it away from him before he .... it!
A chokes B drinks C swallows D chews E gulps

Section B

In this section you will find after each of the passages a number of questions or unfinished statements about the passage, each with four suggested ways of finishing it. You must choose the one which you think fits best. Cross through the letter A, B, C or D for the answer you choose. Give one answer only to each question. Read each passage right through before choosing your answers.

First Passage

Elizabeth and Stephen have not been married very long. They are in Austria and they have met an English boy called Michael, who is on holiday there. He is much younger than they are and they call him their 'son'.

It was about this time that Elizabeth suddenly announced that she would like to go to Salzburg for a couple of days. I was always pleased when she expressed a definite wish of this kind – she so seldom did – and I agreed immediately. To my slight surprise, she suggested taking Michael with us.   5

'I don't want to leave him here by himself,' she explained. 'It sounds silly, I know, but I just cannot bear to think of him being alone. He's such a painfully lonely person, isn't he? It breaks my heart.'

Somehow this didn't sound quite convincing; but I agreed,   10
of course. So to Salzburg we all three went.

I'd supposed, naturally, that this was going to be a holiday

[handwritten top margin] 3.4 Elizabeth asked Stephen to go sight-seeing with Michael and this made Stephen sad but fortunately he didn't show it.

[handwritten left margin] 5. Elizabeth behaved strangely.
6. She was very excited. She had a special piece of news to tell her husband.

for Elizabeth. But the morning after our arrival, she said that
she wanted to work and suggested that I should go sight-seeing
15 with Michael. I was disappointed and even a bit hurt by this,
but I was careful not to show it. Afterwards, I was glad that
I hadn't. *[handwritten] He didn't show it*

At lunch, that day, Elizabeth was in an extraordinary mood. *[handwritten] strange behaviour*
She was gay to the point of silliness and kept making jokes *[handwritten] happy / foolishness*
20 which were quite idiotic.

'What's all the excitement about?' I asked her, as soon as
we were alone together.

'Oh, Stephen, darling, I've been wondering for the last three
hours how I was going to tell you!' Elizabeth threw her arms
25 round my neck and kissed me, laughing. 'And I still don't
know! Perhaps I won't tell you. Perhaps I'll wait till you read
it in the newspapers.'

'Read what, Elizabeth?' I asked, laughing too, though I
didn't know why.

30 'Let me be the first to announce to you, Sir, that I propose to *[handwritten] 見議*
present Michael with a brother. He'd like a brother, wouldn't *[handwritten] (v.)*
he, not a sister? Anyhow, I think I shall insist on a brother.'

'Elizabeth – Oh, my God!' *[handwritten] surprised (astonished)*

'Stephen, you look positively shattered!'

35 'I'm not. No, of course I'm not. I'm delighted. It's only – well,
you know, this takes a bit of getting used to . . . So that was why
you wanted to come here? To see a doctor? And Michael was
to get me out of the way while you did it? But why on earth
didn't you tell me, darling? I'd have gone with you. Is he a good
40 man?'

'One of the best specialists in Austria, I'm told.' *[handwritten] 專家*

'What's his name?'

'Does that matter, darling?'

'I'd like to go and see him myself.'

45 'But, Stephen, whatever for?' *[handwritten] why*

'I just feel I ought to. Doesn't one, usually?'

'Stephen, darling, I'm going to ask you to do something for
me. Will you promise?'

'What is it?'

50 'Promise first.' Elizabeth had become very much in earnest. *[handwritten] (誠懇) 認真地*

'All right, then, I promise.'

'I expect it's terribly female and psychological of me – but *[handwritten] think / very / 心理上 adj*
listen, Stephen. I want you to leave this whole business to me: *[handwritten] thing*
having the baby. I promise faithfully to go to the doctor

32

whenever it's necessary, and do all the things he tells me, and 55
take every precaution. But, somehow, I don't quite know how
to explain it, I want to leave you out of this entirely. I suppose
it's a kind of biological privacy... You've promised, remember?'
'All right,' I said. 'I've promised.'

41 Stephen was pleased that Elizabeth wanted to go to
   Salzburg because
   A   it was only for a couple of days.
   B   it was an opportunity to show Michael the sights of
       Salzburg.
   C   she did not often have any strong desire to do anything.
   D   he wanted to be alone with her.

42 Elizabeth wanted Michael to go to Salzburg with them
   A   because she knew that he was lonely.
   B   but Stephen didn't believe the reason she gave.
   C   and Stephen wanted him to go with them, too.
   D   because she was afraid to leave him behind.

43 Stephen was surprised on arriving in Salzburg
   A   that Elizabeth did not go sight-seeing with him and
       Michael.
   B   because Elizabeth wanted him to work.
   C   that Michael and he had to go sight-seeing.
   D   that Elizabeth disappointed and hurt him.

44 During lunch
   A   Stephen felt a strange excitement.
   B   Elizabeth behaved very strangely.
   C   Elizabeth was moody and idiotic.
   D   Stephen asked Elizabeth what was the matter.

45 Elizabeth was very excited because
   A   she didn't know how to tell Stephen her news.
   B   she had had to wait three hours to tell Stephen her
       news.
   C   something interesting was going to be printed in the
       newspapers.
   D   she had a very special piece of news to tell Stephen.

B

46 Elizabeth told Stephen that
   A   Michael's brother was going to have a present.
   B   Michael wanted a brother and not a sister.
   C   she was going to announce something.
   (D) she was going to have a baby.

47 On hearing Elizabeth's news, Stephen was
   A   shattered and positive.
   (B) pleased and surprised.
   C   uncertain and delighted.
   D   puzzled and frightened.

48 Why had Elizabeth wanted Michael to go to Salzburg with
   them?
   A   To see a doctor.
   B   To go to see the doctor with her.
   (C) To enable her to see the doctor alone.
   D   Not to get in the way of the people at home.

49 Elizabeth did not want Stephen
   A   to know that she was going to have a baby.
   B   to have a baby.
   (C) to see the doctor.
   D   to be left out entirely.

50 Stephen made Elizabeth a promise
   A   but he was not very happy about it.
   B   because Elizabeth was very earnest about it.
   C   when the baby was born.
   (D) before he knew what he was promising.

Second Passage

*The writer, who is nineteen years old, has just arrived in London
for the first time, and is looking for a cheap room.*

It was a large house that stood among other identical large
houses in a tree-shaded square. At first I wondered if there could
be some mistake; the place looked more like the town house of
one of Oscar Wilde's characters. But the address in the ad-
5   vertisement was clear enough, so I rang the doorbell. A coloured
maid answered it. When I said I was looking for a room she
nodded pleasantly, and led me up four flights of stairs.
   The carpets were thick and red, and the wall decorations

34

were of a kind I had only seen in Hollywood musicals. I had a
feeling that I was about to be shown a fifteen-guinea-a-week   10
flat and that I should feel very foolish explaining that I was
looking for something about ten times as cheap. But she led
me up a final narrow flight of stairs (with no carpet, only
linoleum), and showed me a tiny room with a gas-fire, a single
bed, an armchair and a table. It was icy cold.   15

I glanced out of the window at roofs and back gardens, and
asked casually how much it was. She said she would have to
ask the landlady. She led me back to the first floor, where she
rang the bell of an enormous white door with a cut glass knob.
After a long delay, a tall woman in a dressing-gown opened it. 20
She had a beaky nose and the eyes of a bird, and she ignored
me, speaking sharply to the maid: 'Well, Matilda?', like a
headmistress, demanding an explanation.

'This gentleman would like a room, ma'am.'

The sharp eyes now turned on me.   25

'Which one? The top one?'

'The one you advertised,' I explained.

'I have no idea which we advertised,' she said acidly. 'I leave
all that to my agent.'

'The top one, ma'am,' Matilda said.   30

'It's two pounds fifteen a week,' the woman said, surveying
me as if to say 'I am sure this person can't afford it.'

By this time I felt so thoroughly in the wrong that I put on
an overjoyed expression, as if such cheapness surpassed all my
hopes, and said: 'Good. I'd like to take it.'   35

'Can you pay a week in advance?'

'Certainly,' I said, fumbling for my wallet.

She made a little aggrieved motion, and raised her eyebrows
at me. 'Give it to Matilda,' she said, and closed the door on us.

Matilda grinned at me sympathetically, and led me back   40
upstairs. She showed me the location of the bathroom and
lavatory, how to put shillings in the gas meter, and how to light
the gas fire without causing an explosion. Finally she went off
with three pounds, and returned with five shillings and a front
door key. Then I was left alone in my own room at last.   45

51 The writer wondered if there could be some mistake
   because
   A he thought he had mistaken the address.
   B the house did not look like a real one.

C   he did not think he would find a room in that house.

D   it was a very large house in a tree-shaded square.

52 Why did he ring the bell?

    A   Because the address was printed very clearly in the advertisement.

    B   Because he was not sure if he had come to the right house or not.

    C   Because the address of the house was the same as that in the advertisement.

    D   Because he wanted to ask the maid whether he had come to the right house.

53 As he climbed the stairs behind the maid, the writer thought he was going to be

    A   foolish.

    B   stupid.

    C   embarrassed.

    D   disappointed.

54 He thought that the room he was going to see would be

    A   very big and luxurious.

    B   too expensive for him.

    C   tiny and very cold.

    D   at the top of the house.

55 When the landlady opened the door of her flat, she asked the maid

    A   how she was.

    B   if she was well.

    C   what she wanted.

    D   who the man with her was.

56 The writer told the landlady he would take the room because

    A   it was just what he wanted.

    B   it was very cheap.

    C   he was confused by the landlady's behaviour.

    D   he felt it would be wrong to refuse the room.

57 The landlady can best be described as

    A   angry and bad-tempered.

B cold and snobbish.

C suspicious and nervous.

D sharp and sad.

58 Why did Matilda show the writer the location of the bathroom and lavatory?

A Because he didn't know where they were.

B So that he could wash his hands.

C Because he wanted to take a bath.

D Because they were difficult to find.

59 Matilda showed the writer

A how the gas-fire worked.

B where the gas-fire was.

C what the gas-fire was for.

D which gas-fire was his.

60 Why did Matilda come back to the writer's room?

A Because he had given her too much money.

B To give him his change and key.

C Because she had forgotten to give him the key.

D To lock the door.

Test Paper 4

Section A

In this section you must choose the word or phrase which best completes each sentence. Cross through the letter A, B, C, D or E for the word or phrase you choose. Give one answer only for each question.

1   The noise was deafening and we could hardly hear our-selves ....
    A discuss **B** sound **C** say **D** tell **E** speak

2   Why don't you .... your hair cut? You look like an untidy lion.
    A make **B** do **C** get **D** has **E** cut

3   He really is an excellent player. Nobody has ever .... him.
    A won **B** beaten **C** bettered **D** improved **E** led

4   It will be difficult to get tickets, I'm afraid. Have you ....?
    A booked **B** reserved **C** bought **D** ordered
    E occupied

5   For goodness' .... stop asking such silly questions!
    A love **B** like **C** benefit **D** wish **E** sake

6   The soup would be more .... if you had put more meat in it.
    A tasty **B** tasteful **C** tasted **D** tasteless **E** taste

7   The floor was covered with cigarette ends, bits of paper, and all sorts of ....
    A waste **B** rubbish **C** dirt **D** dust **E** stuff

8   May I borrow an iron to .... my trousers?
A smooth   B flatten   C straighten   D stamp   E press

9   Those boys threw a lot of stones at my windows, but
fortunately they broke only one ....
A sheet   B glass   C square   D pane   E panel

10 It is dangerous to lean .... the windows when the train
is moving.
A through   B from   C out by   D out of   E outside

11 The managing director took the .... for the strike,
although it was not really his fault.
A accusation   B guilt   C blame   D punishment
E mistake

12 They .... me a good price for my house, so I sold it.
A showed   B suggested   C brought   D offered
E held out

13 As the sun .... slowly in the west, one by one lights
went on in the houses.
A dropped   B fell   C descended   D sank   E got down

14 We waited for Walter for twenty minutes, and then he
.... looking rather ashamed.
A turned up   B came on   C went in   D broke out
E set up

15 Pat and I had a very enjoyable .... of tennis on Friday
evening.
A play   B game   C match   D test   E fight

16 A .... of £500 has been offered to anyone who finds the
missing pictures.
A reward   B prize   C bribe   D payment   E fee

17 When his Aunt Mildred died, he .... a lot of money.
A got down   B came into   C went over   D turned over
E made off

18 Oh dear! I have .... my purse at home! Will you pay for my ticket, please?
A forgotten B lost C stayed D put E left

19 Did Stella .... her new job when she wrote to you?
A talk B tell C refer D indicate E mention

20 I .... to buy a little house near the sea as soon as I have saved up enough money.
A will B mean C go D can E desire

21 Put the whites of three eggs into a basin, and beat them until they are ....
A rigid B hard C solid D upright E stiff

22 I fell off my bicycle when I was three and I still have a .... on my knee.
A scar B scratch C hole D wound E spot

23 My wife boiled my nylon shirts and they are quite ....
A destroyed B damaged C spoiled D broken E bad

24 I think it would be most .... to invest your money in that company.
A silly B stupid C careless D light E unwise

25 'Have you .... the beds yet, Marian?' 'Yes, Mother, I did them before lunch.'
A seen B prepared C cleaned D made E got

26 The room was full of smoke, but Betty kept her .... and managed to put out the fire.
A mind B head C brain D courage E heart

27 Aspirin is generally .... as the best remedy for a head-ache.
A thought B regarded C considered D valued
E supposed

28 The birds in our garden are very .... and they even come into the sitting-room if we leave the door open.
A quiet B free C tame D peaceful E mild

29 We are trying to .... £4,000 for repairs to the church.
A raise B reach C make D create E gather

30 Parts of the church .... from the eleventh century.
A spring B come C originate D bring E date

31 .... the heavy rain, quite a large crowd of people were
waiting at the station to see the President arrive.
A although B even though C nevertheless
D despite E during

32 Baby is asleep. You may .... at him, but don't wake him
up.
A stare B see C glance D gaze E peep

33 The library is a big one, and there are books to suit all
....
A desires B tastes C ideas D likes E wants

34 The doctor asked me to .... to the waist.
A take off B undress C strip D bare E remove

35 I wish to .... for the post of secretary, advertised in
today's *Daily Blast*.
A apply B ask C propose D write E request

36 I would like to drive across the Sahara Desert next year,
but my wife is not very .... on the idea.
A happy B well C keen D enthusiastic E agreeable

37 Will you accept a cheque or do you prefer .... ?
A money B cash C coins D payment E balance

38 I hear that the men who .... the bank last week have
been arrested.
A robbed B stole C thieved D attacked E took

39 I wouldn't advise you to join the army, Harry. I don't
think you are .... to be a soldier.
A made up B turned out C put down D cut out
E set down

40 Ask Madeleine to help you with those calculations. She
has a good .... for figures.

A brain (B)head C idea D mind E thought

Section B

*In this section, you will find after each of the passages a number
of questions or unfinished statements about the passage, each
with four suggested ways of finishing it. You must choose the
one which you think fits best. Cross through the letter A, B, C
or D for the answer you choose. Give one answer only to each
question. Read each passage right through before choosing your
answer.*

[handwritten: The cook was slightly mad and she regarded all the cooking equipment as her own property]

First Passage
[handwritten: The writer seldom cooked at home.]

When I told my family that I was thinking of taking a cooking
job, the roars of laughter were rather discouraging. No one
believed that I could cook at all, as I had never had a chance to
practise at home. Our cook, aged sixty-five and slightly touched,
5 had ruled in the kitchen for thirty years and had an irritating
tendency to regard the saucepans, stove and indeed all the
kitchen fittings as her own property.

I once crept down there when I thought she was asleep in
her room to try out an omelette. Noiselessly I removed a frying-
10 pan from its hook and the eggs from their cupboard. It was the
pop of the gas that woke her, I think, for I was just breaking
the first egg when a pair of slippered feet shuffled round the
door and a shriek of horror caused me to break the egg on the
floor. This disaster, together with the fact that I was using her
15 one very special beloved and delicately cared-for frying-pan,
upset Cook so much that she locked herself in the larder with
all the food and we had to make our Sunday dinner off bananas.
If the family weren't going to be helpful I would look for a job
all by myself and not tell them about it till I'd got one. I had no
20 idea of exactly what job I should apply for, so I decided to go to
an agency. I had seen one advertised in a local paper, so as soon

[handwritten left margin annotations:
when the writer told her family she wanted to be cook they laugh loudly because she did not have any cooking experience.
The writer can make the cook very angry because she did not like anyone to cook in her kitchen and make it dirty.
She wanted to tell her family after she had found a job. She went to the agency when there was nobody at home.]

42

as there was no one about to say 'Where are you going?' I rushed out of the house in search of it. I was wildly excited, and as nervous as if I were going to a stage audition. Finding the place quite easily, I tore up three flights of stairs, and swung 25 breathlessly through a door which said 'Enter without knocking, if you please'.

The dingy, bottle-green atmosphere of the office sobered me, and I sat meekly on the edge of a chair and could see my nose shining out of the corner of my eye. I thought perhaps it was a 30 good thing; it might look more earnest. The woman at the desk opposite scrutinized me for a while through rimless glasses, and I became absorbed in the question of whether or not she wore a wig. I had just decided that it was too undesirably shabby to be anything but her own hair, when I realized that 35 she was murmuring questions at me. I answered in a hoarse whisper because it seemed to be the thing, and because all of a sudden I started to feel rather pathetic. She hinted in a delicate way that she wondered why I was looking for this sort of job, so I felt impelled to give her a glimpse of a widowed mother and 40 a desperate struggle against poverty. I almost made myself believe in the pathos of it, and we had to cough and change the subject. I felt even more pathetic when she told me that it would be difficult to get a job without experience or references. She rustled about among her papers for a bit and I wondered 45 whether I ought to leave, when the telephone on her desk rang. While she was conducting a mysterious conversation she kept looking at me. Then I heard her say:

'As a matter of fact, I've got someone in the office at this very moment, who might suit.' She wrote down a number, and my 50 spirits soared as I took the slip of paper she held out to me, saying: 'Ring up this lady. She wants a cook immediately. In fact, you would have to start tomorrow by cooking dinner for ten people. Could you manage that, I wonder?'

'Oh yes,' said I – never having cooked for more than four in 55 my life.

41 The writer's family laughed when she told them that she was thinking of taking a cooking job because
  A she had never cooked anything at home.
  B she had said this as a joke.
  C they knew that she was a very bad cook.
  D they wanted to discourage her from the idea.

43

42 The cook was angry and upset because
    A the writer had broken an egg on the kitchen floor.
    B she didn't like anyone else to cook in her kitchen.
    C the writer had not asked her if she might use her frying-pan.
    D she had been woken up from her sleep by a noise in the kitchen.

43 The writer decided to
    A look for a job because her family were not helpful.
    B find a job and not tell her family about it.
    C tell her family only after she had found a job.
    D give up the idea of finding a job.

44 She waited until there was no one about because
    A she did not want to tell anyone where she was going.
    B she thought her family might stop her from going.
    C she did not know where the agency was.
    D she was very excited and nervous.

45 She was breathless when she arrived at the office because
    A she was excited and nervous.
    B she had run up a lot of stairs.
    C she had not told the family where she was going.
    D she needed a job very badly.

46 The writer thought that the woman in the office
    A was wearing a shabby wig.
    B had very unattractive hair.
    C had a wig because her hair was unattractive.
    D should wear a wig to hide her hair.

47 The writer answered the woman's questions in a whisper because
    A she wanted to make her believe her story.
    B she was very nervous and excited.
    C the woman spoke very softly to her.
    D she wanted to make the woman think she was pathetic.

48 The woman told the writer that it would be difficult to get a job because
    A she did not know how to cook.

    B she was so pathetic.

    C her references were not good enough.

    (D) she had never had a job before.

49 A lady telephoned the agency
    A to ask them to cook a dinner for ten people.
    B because she wanted the writer to ring her up.
    C because she was not able to cook a dinner for ten people.
    (D) because she needed a cook to start work at once.

50 When the writer said 'Oh yes' (line 55) she meant that
    A she would ring the lady up.
    (B) she was able to cook a dinner for ten people.
    C she would be able to start work the next day.
    D she could start work immediately.

Second Passage

I am going to tell you about rather a curious experience I had
three years ago. One morning in October a letter arrived by the
first post which rather puzzled me. The envelope was type-
written and it contained just a single stall for Wyndham's
Theatre for the same evening. No letter or card to say who it   5.
was from – just the ticket.
   Of course, it was obvious what had happened – somebody
had found himself with a ticket that he could not use and had
sent it on to me, quite forgetting to put a note in with it. He
would probably ring me up during the morning. However, no   10
one did telephone, so during the afternoon I got through to
two people who might have sent it, but neither of them had.
Anyway, it didn't matter. The play was *Bulldog Drummond*,
and I hadn't seen it, so I naturally decided to go.
   I got there a shade early and went and sat in my seat, which   15
was in the middle of the sixth row, wondering rather vaguely
which of my friends was going to sit next to me; at the moment
there was no one else in the row at all. Presently in came four
Americans who took the seats to my left – not people I knew –
and a minute or two later an elderly married couple, whom I   20
did not know either, came in and sat down next but one to my
right. When the curtain went up the seat immediately to my
right was still empty, and so it was at the end of the act.
During the first interval I went out and smoked a cigarette,

45

He had gone out during the first and second interval.
At the last act the seat ~~was~~ occupied by an attractive lady whom the
writer did not know ^appeared^

25   and during the second – as still no one had turned up to sit in
the seat – I went round to the box office and asked whether it
had been sold at all. 'Oh yes,' said the girl; it had been sold all
right and to the same person who had bought mine the day
before, but that was all she could tell me. So I didn't worry any
30   more.

    Now, then. While I was ^pulling~~clawing~~^ my way back to my seat for
the last act the lights went down, but there was just enough
twilight left to see that the mysterious stall was at last occupied
– and by a lady whom I had never seen before in my life. I must
35   describe her a little, if you don't mind, because her appearance
had everything to do with what happened afterwards.

    She was about thirty. Most attractive-looking and well
turned out. She hadn't much jewellery, but what there was
looked good. I liked the way she did her hair; I mean it was
40   ^well^ properly dressed. None of your last year's birds' nests which
you so often see at the theatre. I am afraid I am not much good
at describing people, but speaking quite generally – well – she
was the sort of woman who looks you straight in the face and
says 'Thank you' when you give her your seat in the Tube. In
45   fact, rather unusual.

The lady charming and well dressed she was frank and polite

51   The writer was puzzled (line 3) because
    A   the envelope was typewritten.
    (B) there was no letter in the envelope.
    C   he wasn't expecting to receive a letter.
    D   the envelope had a theatre ticket in it.

52   The writer thought that
    (A) the theatre ticket was a present from someone who
          had not been able to use it.
    B   somebody had sent the ticket to him by mistake, and
         this worried him.
    C   somebody had sent him a theatre ticket unexpectedly
         and he did not know what to do with it.
    D   the theatre ticket had been put into his letter by mis-
         take and he should return it.

53   During the morning, the writer expected
    A   a man to telephone him to ask about the ticket.
    B   to be telephoned about a note which had been
         forgotten.

She was attractive, well dressed, frank and polite

C to telephone somebody about the ticket.

D the sender of the theatre ticket to telephone him.

54 During the afternoon, the writer telephoned two people and said

    A 'Why have you sent me a theatre ticket?'

    B 'Thank you very much for sending me a theatre ticket.'

    C 'I have received the theatre ticket that you sent me.'

    D 'Have you sent me a theatre ticket?'

55 When he arrived at the theatre, the writer

    A thought he would find out who had sent him the ticket.

    B sat in the sixth row next to some Americans.

    C did not see anyone that he knew.

    D waited for the person who had sent him the theatre ticket.

56 During the intervals, the writer

    A left his seat.

    B smoked cigarettes.

    C went to the box office.

    D didn't worry.

57 While the writer was going back to his seat after the second interval

    A a lady arrived.

    B it became dark.

    C he didn't worry.

    D he recognized somebody.

58 A lady sat down in the empty stall

    A during the last act.

    B during the second interval.

    C while the writer was smoking a cigarette.

    D while the writer was making his way back to his seat.

59 The writer says that the lady was

    A well-dressed and attractive.

    B richly-dressed and mysterious.

    C strange and unknown.

    D about thirty but good.

60 The writer says that the lady was 'rather unusual' (line 45)
because
A   her hair was neatly dressed.
B   she looked him straight in the face.
C   she was about thirty.
D   she had a frank and sincere look.

Test Paper 5

Section A

In this section you must choose the word or phrase which best completes each sentence. Cross through the letter A, B, C, D or E for the word or phrase you choose. Give one answer only for each question.

1   It's a very .... little car. It doesn't use much petrol, and it's easy to park.
    A comfortable   **B** cheap   **C** convenient   **D** handy
    E easy

2   What's the matter with you? You look as if you had seen a ....
    A monster   **B** sight   **C** ghost   **D** tragedy   **E** horror

3   I .... not tell my mother what I have done. She will be furious.
    A ought   **B** should   **C** could   **D** will   **E** dare

4   I have been working since six o'clock this morning, and I am absolutely ....
    A tired   **B** destroyed   **C** exhausted   **D** down   **E** through

5   You've managed to find a flat? What a .... of luck!
    A stroke   **B** blow   **C** touch   **D** fortune   **E** kind

6   We managed to catch a .... of the Queen as the procession passed.
    A sight   **B** view   **C** spectacle   **D** glance   **E** glimpse

7   This book is much too difficult for me; most of it is quite .... my comprehension.
    A over   **B** beyond   **C** outside   **D** further than
    E through

49

8 Ours is a .... village, and some of the houses are in very lonely positions.
   A long B scattered C extended D spread E diffused

9 The cemetery is on the .... of the town, near the road that leads to the motorway.
   A suburbs B outside C surroundings D outskirts
   E neighbourhood

10 Aunt Emma is coming for lunch. Please .... the room before she arrives.
   A tidy B order C arrange D polish E set out

11 How can we get in .... with Herbert? He is not on the phone.
   A talk B speak C communicate D touch
   E conversation

12 Once winter has really .... we shan't be able to cross the mountain pass.
   A turned up B gone on C come out D set in
   E fallen down

13 Uncle Henry was a tall serious man who said ....
   A a little B much C little D few E many

14 He was highly .... as a doctor.
   A seen B considered C thought of D estimated
   E valued

15 No .... lights are allowed anywhere near the petrol tanks.
   A bare B naked C nude D plain E uncovered

16 .... what you say, I am convinced that I am right.
   A no matter B doesn't matter C no importance
   D never mind E no difference

17 At the end of the dinner, the president rose to make a ....
   A declaration B talk C lecture D speech
   E commentary

18 'Why didn't you ask me to help you?' 'It never .... to me!'
A happened B occurred C thought D entered E fell

19 The sack was far too heavy for me to carry, so I .... it across the floor.
A drew B trained C trailed D dragged E threw

20 Please go away and leave me in ....!
A calm B quiet C peace D solitude E silence

21 Although the book shows no .... of imagination, it is very carelessly written.
A lack B shortage C weakness D want E scarceness

22 The unpleasant customs official .... on my opening all my cases.
A suggested B asked C determined D repeated E insisted

23 I thought Harriet might have been disturbed by the noise, but she was .... asleep.
A fast B quite C completely D off E full

24 I have lost so much weight recently that all my clothes are too big; I must have them ....
A put down B let out C taken in D cut off E made out

25 Michael is very selfish and has no .... for the feelings of other people.
A attention B interest C feeling D regard E mind

26 Go and play in the garden, Roger, and don't be a ....
A trouble B care C bother D nuisance E headache

27 Uncle William has bought a piece of .... near the sea and he is going to build a house there.
A earth B soil C territory D land E country

28 When I started work I gave my first week's .... to my mother.
A salary B income C fees D wages E cash

51

29 Janet is in bed with a .... attack of flu.
    A hard   B severe   C strict   D heavy   E large

30 My garden gives me great ...., especially in spring-time.
    A pleasure   B liking   C enjoying   D appreciation
    E benefit

31 .... writers are as well known as Shakespeare.
    A some   B a lot of   C many   D few   E little

32 The policeman on the corner looked very important, and
    Sally was too .... to ask him the way to the station.
    A shy   B reserved   C quiet   D young   E afraid

33 Admission to the museum is .... except on Sundays and
    holidays, when a charge of 15p is made.
    A nothing   B allowed   C paid   D given   E free

34 Will you .... a seat for a few moments, please? Mr Hall
    will see you shortly.
    A sit on   B make   C take   D look for   E hold

35 Emily is a terrible .... and if you tell her anything the
    whole village will know it within a few hours.
    A shouter   B gossip   C talker   D liar   E speaker

36 We hurried as much as we could, as we were .... to
    reach the village before the storm broke.
    A eager   B hopeful   C contented   D worried   E wanted

37 Barbara is one of the thinnest girls I have ever seen, but
    her sister Kate is even thinner ....
    A again   B more   C yet   D still   E worse

38 The woman next door has been playing the violin since
    three o'clock this afternoon, and I just can't .... it any
    longer.
    A hold   B support   C do with   D have   E bear

39 She was .... by her grandmother because her parents
    had died when she was a baby.
    A taken out   B brought up   C educated   D seen to
    E let in

52

40 The letters M.P. .... Member of Parliament, or, more
rarely, Military Police.

A mean B stand as C signify D want to say
E stand for

Section B

*In this section, you will find after each of the passages a number
of questions or unfinished statements about the passage, each
with four suggested ways of finishing it. You must choose the
one which you think fits best. Cross through the letter A, B, C
or D for the answer you choose. Give one answer only to each
question. Read each passage right through before choosing your
answer.*

First Passage

We found the right bar at last. I didn't have to ask again, for
there it was in big red neon letters over the window – Star Bar.
There were some iron tables outside with plastic chairs around
them and tired-looking dusty shrubs in pots here and there.
A few people sat listlessly around, looking at a portable   5
television set that someone had brought out of the bar. They
were all in thin summer dresses or short-sleeved shirts; even
at that late hour the heat was stifling. Two thin dogs lay under
one of the tables with their tongues out, and some of the women
were fanning themselves unenthusiastically with magazines.   10
 'He's not here,' I said, after a quick look round. The television
was blaring out an advertisement for a detergent, and the people
sitting round had their eyes glued to the picture of a woman
proudly showing how white her husband's underwear was after
having been washed in Sludge. They took no notice of us at all. 15
 'Well, what did you expect?' replied Fergus, yawning. 'It's
only half past nine, and he said he would be here at nine. You
ought to know Craig by this time. He'll turn up sometime after
ten.'
 We sat down at one of the vacant tables, and gazed at the   20
television in company with the other customers. The ad-
vertisements were over now and a fairly young woman with
an incredible number of large white teeth was telling us what
we would be able to have the pleasure of seeing later that
evening. There was no sign of movement among the people at   25

53

the tables except for the pessimistic fanning of the women. One of the thin dogs started to scratch and then decided that it was not worth the effort and stopped.

'If you want a drink, you'll have to go in and get it,' said
30 Fergus, studying his finger-nails. 'Obviously nobody is going to come and ask us what we want.'

'Don't you want a drink?' I asked.

'Yes, but not sufficiently to go to the trouble of going in to order it.'

35 I got to my feet, and as I pushed my chair back the metal feet grated loudly on the pavement, but nobody even glanced in my direction. I could have taken out a gun and shot myself and nobody would have paid the slightest attention.

Inside the bar it was cooler than outside, and at the end of
40 the counter a pale fat youth was leaning against the coffee machine, reading the sports section of the evening paper. A cigarette drooped from his lip, and as he raised his eyebrows at me in an inquiring gesture, the ash dropped from the end of it and fell into the sugar basin.

45 I held up two fingers.

He nodded, took two bottles from the fridge and held them up to me with another inquiring look. I nodded. I wondered if he was dumb or whether it was just too much effort to speak. He opened the bottles and poured the beer into glasses in
50 silence and I paid and pocketed my change in silence too. Then the fat boy lit another cigarette and took up his stance at the coffee machine again.

'You'd better go back and get another one,' said Fergus, yawning again, when I reached our table with the two brimming
55 glasses. 'Craig has just come round the corner of the street.'

41 The writer and his friend
    A had never been to that bar before.
    B didn't know if they had come to the right place.
    C asked somebody the name of the bar.
    D had little difficulty in finding the bar.

42 The people outside the bar
    A were very interested in the television programme.
    B didn't care if someone committed suicide.
    C had no particular interest in anything
    D were very hot and uncomfortable.

54

43 Why did the writer and Fergus go to the Star Bar?
    A To keep an appointment with Craig.
    B In the hope of finding Craig there.
    C Because Craig had said that he might be there.
    D Because Craig was usually there in the evening.

44 It was a very hot evening although
    A the customers of the bar were sitting outside.
    B the people were wearing light summer clothes.
    C it was half past nine.
    D it was autumn.

45 Fergus was not surprised that Craig was not there, because
    he knew that
    A Craig intended to come later.
    B they had mistaken the time.
    C Craig had been delayed.
    D Craig was always late.

46 Craig and the other two men
    A were very old friends.
    B did not like each other much.
    C had to discuss business together.
    D had known each other a long time.

47 The writer had to go into the bar because
    A he was very thirsty.
    B there was no waiter outside.
    C Fergus wanted a drink.
    D it was cooler there than outside.

48 What does the passage tell us about Fergus?
    A He was tired.
    B He was thirsty.
    C He was lazy.
    D He did not like that bar.

49 The writer and the fat boy in the bar
    A didn't understand each other's language.
    B had very little conversation.
    C managed to make themselves understood.
    D didn't like each other.

50 The writer had to buy another beer because
    A Craig had arrived.
    B Craig hadn't arrived.
    C Craig was about to arrive.
    D Craig might arrive.

Second Passage

Even medical students must have somewhere to live. The problem of finding suitable accommodation is difficult because they
are always disinclined to spend on mere food and shelter money
that would do equally well for beer and tobacco. And they are
5   not, as a rule, popular lodgers. They always sit up late, they
come in drunk on Saturdays, and they have queer things in
bottles in their bedrooms. On the other hand, there are a small
number of landladies who think it a privilege to entertain a
prospective doctor under their roof. The connection with the
10 profession raises their social standing in the street, and the
young gentlemen can always be consulted over the dinner
table on the strictly private illnesses to which landladies seem
distressingly liable.

I started off in lodgings in Finchley, which were clean, fairly
15 cheap and comfortable. The landlady had a daughter, a tall
blank-faced brunette of nineteen, an usherette at the local
cinema. One evening after I had been there about six weeks she
tapped at my bedroom door.

'Are you in bed?' she asked anxiously.
20 'No,' I called through the door. 'I'm studying. What is it?'
'It's my foot,' she said. 'I think I've sprained it or something.
Will you have a look at it for me?'
'In the kitchen,' I replied guardedly. 'Take your stocking off
and I'll be down in a minute.'
25 The following week she developed a pain in the calf, and the
one after stiffness of the knee. When she knocked on the door
and complained of a bad hip I gave notice.

I moved into a top-floor room of a lodging-house near Paddington Station. Its residents represented so many nationalities
30 the directions for working its tricky and uncertain lavatories
had to be set up in four different languages, as in the Conti-
nental expresses. There was another medical student there, a
man from St. Mary's Hospital, who kept tropical fish in a tank
in his bedroom and practised Yogi.
35 As I had to take all my meals out I saw little of the other

56

lodgers except when they passed on the stairs and said 'Excuse me' in bad English. In the room next to mine was a stout young blonde, but she lived very quietly and never disturbed anyone. One morning she was found strangled in Hyde Park and after that I thought I ought to move again.   40

For the following twelve months I lived in a succession of boarding-houses. They were all the same. They had a curly hat-stand in the hall, a red stair-carpet worn grey in the middle, and a suspicious landlady. By the time I reached the end of the anatomy course I was tired of the smell of floor-polish,   45 damp umbrellas, and frying; when I was offered a share in a flat in Bayswater I was so delighted I packed up and moved without even waiting to work out the week's rent.

51 It is difficult for medical students to find accommodation
    because
    A they are usually very poor and cannot afford to pay
       much.
    B they are unpopular people.
    C they prefer to spend their money on other things.
    D they keep bottles in their bedrooms.

52 Some landladies like to have medical students as lodgers
    because
    A they can discuss their illnesses during meals.
    B medical students are sociable people.
    C they feel safer with a doctor in the house.
    D medical students are specially privileged people.

53 The writer left his lodgings in Finchley because
    A the landlady's daughter was always very ill.
    B he couldn't study there very well.
    C he was afraid of having trouble with the landlady's
       daughter.
    D the landlady's daughter was always knocking on his
       door.

54 In the house in Paddington
    A the lavatories were international.
    B it was difficult to understand how the lavatories
       worked.
    C there were four different lavatories for different
       nationalities.
    D the writer was uncertain how to work the lavatory.

55 In the house in Paddington
  A there were a lot of medical students from different countries.
  B there were two medical students.
  C most of the lodgers were studying English.
  D the lodgers were all students.

56 The writer
  A was not able to eat in his room.
  B preferred eating in restaurants.
  C used to take sandwiches out with him.
  D never ate anything in his room.

57 What made the writer decide to leave the house in Paddington?
  A The bad English of the other lodgers.
  B The stout young blonde in the next room.
  C The death of his next-door neighbour.
  D The fact that he had to eat out.

58 The boarding-houses that the writer lived in during the next year were
  A damp and smelly.
  B suspicious.
  C uncomfortable.
  D alike.

59 When he had finished his anatomy course
  A he bought a flat in Bayswater.
  B he went to live in a flat with some other people.
  C someone asked him if he wanted to take a flat in Bayswater.
  D he thought he would like to take a flat in Bayswater.

60 He moved into a flat
  A and didn't pay the last week's rent for his lodgings.
  B and worked instead of paying rent.
  C but hadn't calculated how much the rent would be.
  D after a good deal of consideration.

Test Paper 6

Section A

In this section you must choose the word or phrase which best completes each sentence. Cross through the letter A, B, C, D or E for the word or phrase you choose. Give one answer only for each question.

1   I think there is something wrong with that lamp. I .... a shock when I tried to switch it on.
    A took **B** had **C** got **D** made **E** felt

2   .... where you go, prices are higher than they were last year.
    A doesn't matter **B** in every **C** no importance
    D in any case **E** no matter

3   Put the lid back on the tin so that the biscuits .... crisp and fresh.
    A become **B** make **C** get **D** keep **E** bring

4   After shouting with such enthusiasm at the football match, Adam was so .... the next day that he could hardly speak.
    A tired **B** bad **C** weak **D** hoarse **E** faint

5   My mother died when I was at school, and now my father has just married again, and my .... is younger than I am!
    A stepmother **B** mother-in-law **C** godmother
    D foster mother **E** motherhood

6   Oh look! There's a wedding on at that church. Let's wait and see the .... arrive.
    A woman **B** spouse **C** wife **D** bride **E** marriage

59

7   .... all my friends have moved away from this area and
     I feel rather lonely.
     A surely   **B** certainly   **C** practically   **D** normally
     E sadly

8   Brian is wearing a blue and yellow .... tie that his
     girl-friend gave him.
     A lined   **B** striped   **C** designed   **D** pictured   **E** barred

9   Uncle Charlie is completely .... so he prefers to keep
     his hat on wherever he goes.
     A naked   **B** hairy   **C** bare   **D** bald   **E** smooth

10   They .... my letter by return of post.
     A acknowledged   **B** thanked   **C** wrote   **D** posted
     E registered

11   While gathering some roses, she hurt her finger on a
     ....
     A point   **B** thorn   **C** pin   **D** nail   **E** spine

12   On my desk there is a photograph in a silver .... of my
     wife and family.
     A edge   **B** box   **C** frame   **D** case   **E** holder

13   This knife is terribly .... It won't even cut a piece of
     cheese.
     A flat   **B** sharp   **C** thick   **D** old   **E** blunt

14   Wait a moment. I must just .... a note for my husband.
     A draw   **B** create   **C** scribble   **D** design   **E** pencil

15   I didn't really understand what the writer was ....
     A getting at   **B** looking for   **C** making for   **D** doing to
     E trying out

16   That hotel was built .... as an office-block.
     A originally   **B** once   **C** first   **D** formerly
     E occasionally

17   We can't play with this pack of cards; the king of spades
     and the four of hearts are ....
     A absent   **B** departed   **C** missing   **D** lacking   **E** going

60

18 Uncle Rupert was .... in the First World War.
A damaged   B destroyed   C broken   D wounded 傷口
(E) injured 受傷

19 That vase is very old and valuable; please .... it carefully.
A place   (B) handle   C drop   D treat   E make

20 A Prime Minister has to .... very great responsibilities.
A head   B back   C chest   (D) shoulder   E hand

21 Can I .... Birmingham direct from here, or must I ask
the exchange to get the number for me?
A select   B reach   C choose   D dial   E speak

22 I had to .... the invitation as I had a previous engagement.
A forget   B abandon   C refuse   D deny   E leave

23 The street lamps are switched on automatically at ....
A dusk   B dark   C black   D sunrise   E evening

24 Five people were badly .... when a bus ran into a wall.
A wounded   B killed   C damaged   D broken   E hurt

25 The Post Office Tower .... slightly in the wind.
A bends   B bows   C curves   D leans   E sways

26 I found my daughter sitting in the kitchen, crying ....
A heavily   B bitterly   C deeply   D strongly   E greatly
難過地

27 My telephone is .... so I shall have to ask my neighbour
if I can use his.
A out of order   B on strike   C off limits   D off duty
E out of use

28 So far, the police have been able to find no .... of the
missing documents.
A piece   B evidence   C indication   D help   E trace

29 She .... of severe pains in her arms and legs.
A remarks   B says   C notices   D grumbles
E complains

61

30 She put her head on my shoulder and I .... her hair
gently.
A rubbed   B washed   C pulled   D stroked   E knocked

31 .... your coat. The wind is very cold today.
A do up   B put off   C take on   D put in   E make up

32 The driver saw the red light at the very last moment, and
with a squeal of .... the lorry stopped just in time.
A people   B wheels   C brakes   D policemen   E noise

33 The soup is terribly .... You put far too much pepper
in it.
A strong   B hot   C thick   D dark   E tasty

34 Don't forget to put the .... on the toothpaste when you
have finished with it.
A cap   B lid   C cover   D end   E hat

35 My brother will never be rich; he spends money like ....
A beer   B waste   C Scotsmen   D water   E bread

36 When you arrive in England with your car, remember to
.... to the left.
A turn   B keep   C hold   D go   E drive

37 The mysterious woman was dressed .... in black.
A all over   B from top to bottom   C from end to end
D from head to foot   E back to front

38 Aunt Harriet was .... by a wasp while she was gathering
some plums.
A bitten   B eaten   C stung   D wounded   E pricked

39 The car suddenly stopped, and I realized that we had ....
of petrol.
A gone off   B run out   C finished   D used up
E come down

40 .... you will have to make up your mind, so you might
as well do it now.
A sooner or later   B first and foremost   C first of all
D after all   E last of all

62

Section B

In this section you will find after each passage a number of questions or unfinished statements, each with four suggested ways of finishing it. You must choose the one which you think fits best. Cross through the letter A, B, C or D for the answer you choose. Give one answer only to each question. Read each passage right through before choosing your answers.

First Passage

Billy Weaver had travelled down from London on the slow afternoon train, with a change at Swindon on the way, and by the time he got to Bath it was about nine o'clock in the evening and the moon was coming up out of a clear starry sky over the houses opposite the station entrance. But the air was deadly 5 cold and the wind was like a flat blade of ice on his cheeks.

'Excuse me,' he said, 'but is there a fairly cheap hotel not too far away from here?'

'Try The Bell and Dragon,' the porter answered, pointing down the road. 'They might take you in. It's about a quarter of 10 a mile along on the other side.'

Billy thanked him and picked up his suitcase and set out to walk the quarter-mile to The Bell and Dragon. He had never been to Bath before. He didn't know anyone who lived there. But Mr Greenslade at the Head Office in London had told him 15 it was a splendid city.

'Find your own lodgings,' he had said, 'and report to the Branch Manager as soon as you've got yourself settled.'

Billy was seventeen years old. He was wearing a new navy-blue overcoat, a new brown trilby hat, and a new brown suit, 20 and he was feeling fine. He walked briskly down the street. He was trying to do everything briskly these days. Briskness, he had decided, was the one common characteristic of all successful businessmen. The big shots up at Head Office were absolutely fantastically brisk all the time. They were amazing. 25

There were no shops on this wide street that he was walking along, only a line of tall houses on each side, all of them identical. They had porches and pillars and four or five steps going up to their front doors, and it was obvious that once upon a time they had been very high-class residences. But now, even 30 in the darkness, he could see that the paint was peeling from the woodwork on their doors and windows, and that the handsome white façades were cracked and discoloured from neglect.

35   Suddenly, in a downstairs window that was brilliantly illuminated by a street-lamp not six yards away, Billy caught sight of a printed notice propped up against the glass in one of the upper panes. It said 'Bed and Breakfast'.

41   Billy Weaver
    A   stopped at Bath on the way to Swindon.
    B   had to change trains before arriving in Swindon.
    C   came to Bath from Swindon by train.
    D   was late arriving in Swindon and had to change.

42   When he arrived in Bath
    A   it was snowing.
    B   it was a fine day.
    C   the weather was cold.
    D   it was dark and wet.

43   What happened when he arrived?
    A   He asked a porter the way to The Bell and Dragon hotel.
    B   The porter told him he had to go to The Bell and Dragon.
    C   He asked the porter for accommodation near the station.
    D   He asked the porter to find him a room not far from the station.

44   The porter told Billy that
    A   The Bell and Dragon was a long way from the station.
    B   The Bell and Dragon might have a room but he was not sure.
    C   The Bell and Dragon would be a very good hotel to stay at.
    D   The Bell and Dragon would probably charge him too much.

45   Billy's orders from Head Office were to
    A   ask the Branch Manager to find him somewhere to live.
    B   go to see the Branch Manager as soon as he arrived.
    C   settle in Bath because it was a splendid city.
    D   look for somewhere to live before doing anything else.

46 Why did Billy Weaver go to Bath?
   A For a holiday.
   B On a business trip.
   C To look for a job.
   D To take up a job.

47 Billy walked in a particular way because
   A he wanted to impress people who were brisk in their movements.
   B he wanted to move quickly in order not to waste time.
   C he wanted to imitate the people who worked at Head Office.
   D he would have liked to have been able to do everything briskly.

48 The houses in the street
   A were not as big as they appeared to be at first.
   B were all exactly the same.
   C were grand and elegant.
   D had not been painted.

49 Why did Billy catch sight of the notice?
   A Because it was in the window.
   B Because it was clearly printed.
   C Because there was a street-lamp close by.
   D Because he was looking for such a notice.

50 Where was the notice?
   A At the bottom of the window.
   B Outside the downstairs window.
   C Inside a window.
   D At one of the upper windows.

Second Passage

Harriet Vane is in Oxford, and has been invited by Lord Saint George to have lunch with him in his college.

Harriet drove down St. Aldgate's on Monday and inquired of the porter beneath Tom Tower for Lord Saint George; only to be told that Lord Saint George was not in College.

'Oh!' said Harriet, disconcerted, 'but he asked me to lunch.'

'What a pity they didn't let you know, Miss. Lord Saint   5

c   65

George was in a nasty motor-accident on Friday night. He's in the Infirmary. Didn't you see it in the papers?'

'No, I missed it. Is he badly hurt?'

10 'Injured his shoulder and cut his head open pretty badly, so we hear,' said the porter, with regret, and yet, with a slight relish at the imparting of bad news. 'He was unconscious for twenty-four hours; but we are informed that his condition is now improving. The Duke and Duchess have left for the country again.'

15 'Dear me!' said Harriet. 'I'm sorry to hear this. I'd better go round and inquire. Do you know whether he is allowed to see anybody yet?'

The porter looked her over with a paternal eye, which somehow suggested to her that if she had been an under-
20 graduate the answer would have been 'No'.

'I believe, Miss,' said the porter, 'that Mr Danvers and Lord Warboys were permitted to visit his lordship this morning. I couldn't say further than that. Excuse me – there is Mr Danvers just crossing the quadrangle. I will ascertain.'

25 He emerged from his glass case and pursued Mr Danvers, who immediately came running to the lodge.

'I say,' said Mr Danvers, 'are you Miss Vane? Because poor old Saint George has only just remembered about you. He's terribly sorry, and I was to catch you and give you some lunch.
30 No trouble at all – a great pleasure. We ought to have let you know, but he was knocked clean out, poor chap. And then, what with the family fussing round – do you know the Duchess? – No? – Ah! – Well, she went off this morning, and then I was allowed to go round and got my instructions. Terrific apologies
35 and all that.'

'How did it happen?'

'Driving a racing car to the danger of the public,' said Mr Danvers.

51 The porter told Harriet that it was a pity that
    A she had come because Lord Saint George was not there.
    B nobody had told her the news of the accident.
    C she had not gone to the Infirmary.
    D Lord Saint George had had an accident.

52 Harriet didn't know about the accident because
    A she didn't read newspapers as a rule.

B she had not been able to buy a newspaper.

C she had been too late to read a newspaper.

D she had not seen the report of the accident.

53 The porter
  A rather enjoyed telling Harriet the details of the accident.
  B told Harriet that Lord Saint George was only slightly hurt.
  C regretted having to tell Harriet the details of the accident.
  D was sorry that Lord Saint George had been unconscious.

54 Harriet asked the porter
  A which hospital Lord Saint George was in.
  B whether Lord Saint George was well enough to see visitors.
  C if Lord Saint George wanted her to go and visit him.
  D if she had better go and visit Lord Saint George in hospital.

55 Why did the porter not say 'No' to Harriet? (line 20)
  A Because he felt sorry for her.
  B Because he liked the look of her.
  C Because she was evidently not a student.
  D Because he felt fatherly towards her.

56 The porter ran after Mr Danvers to ask him
  A if Harriet could visit Lord Saint George.
  B if Lord Saint George was conscious yet.
  C how Lord Saint George was after the accident.
  D whether the Duke and Duchess had gone away.

57 Mr Danvers asked Harriet
  A if she wanted to have lunch with Lord Saint George.
  B why she had come to Lord Saint George's college.
  C if she would visit Lord Saint George in hospital.
  D if she would have lunch with him.

58 Lord Saint George had been unconscious, so
  A he did not know he had had an accident.
  B he could not let Harriet know he had had an accident.

C he could not tell anyone he had asked Harriet to come for lunch.

D the Duke and Duchess had gone back to the country again.

59 Mr Danvers had seen Lord Saint George
   A in hospital, immediately after the accident.
   B after the Duke and the Duchess had left.
   C because Lord Saint George had asked to see him.
   D during lunch.

60 We get the impression that
   A the Duchess was very worried about her son's accident.
   B Mr Danvers was very fond of the Duchess.
   C the Duchess was a difficult woman.
   D the Duchess liked Mr Danvers.

Test Paper 7

Section A

In this section you must choose the word or phrase which best completes each sentence. Cross through the letter A, B, C, D or E for the word or phrase you choose. Give one answer only for each question.

1   Six oranges, two grapefruit and a small .... of grapes, please.
    A group   B mass   C cluster   D bunch   E heap

2   I love to .... round the old part of the town, enjoying its peace and quiet.
    A rush   B sit   C wait   D wander   E tour

3   Don't forget to take all the .... out of the cherries when you cook them.
    A seeds   B stones   C nuts   D pips   E grounds

4   Oh, what a ....! The bank is already closed, and I want to draw some money out.
    A trouble   B bother   C curse   D annoyance
    E nuisance

5   I have complete confidence in him; he is absolutely ....
    A good   B reliable   C dependent   D trustful   E fine

6   Harry had an unfortunate experience at the Carnival Ball. His false moustache .... fire as he was lighting a cigarette.
    A caught   B took   C made   D lit   E reached

7   Sue and Bill are quite .... now, but they were very poor when they first married.
    A right   B well done   C overpaid   D for the best
    E well off

8   Cowboys used to be employed to look after the ....
     A beasts   B animals   C cattle   D creatures   E cows

9   When I started work, many years ago, I only .... £1 a
     week.
     A took   B stole   C paid   D got   E put

10   Barbara .... that she was pleased to see us, but she was
     really quite angry that we had arrived.
     A took on   B put down   C set in   D let by   E made out

11   The .... purpose of our visit was to deliver a message
     from Uncle Bert.
     A main   B greatest   C large   D supreme   E important

12   The windscreen was covered with ice, and I tried to ....
     it off with my fingers.
     A pull   B cut   C scrape   D draw   E grab

13   If .... you hadn't been so foolish as to lose the key!
     A but   B as   C unless   D though   E only

14   The .... of our friends are young married couples,
     like us.
     A most   B majority   C many   D greatest   E average

15   Can you help me? I can't .... how to start this machine.
     A find out   B get on   C set down   D tell off   E do in

16   Mrs Fielding was wearing a strange black hat with a
     long .... in it.
     A fur   B hair   C piece   D feather   E tail

17   'Did you go to the casino when you were on holiday?'
     'No, I never ....'
     A gamble   B bet   C play   D hazard   E try

18   I could hear the .... of dishes in the kitchen; Sarah was
     washing up.
     A squeak   B shout   C jingle   D rustle   E clatter

19   Evelyn kicked me hard on the .... to warn me not to say
     anything more.
     A toe   B ankle   C elbow   D knee   E neck

70

20 Don't swallow that chewing-gum! .... it out!
   A drop B spit C splash D chew E send

21 Uncle Albert came to the party wearing a shabby old suit,
   worn-out shoes and no socks. There was a big hole in his
   trousers. He looked just like a ....
   A criminal B prisoner C tramp D passenger
   E merchant.

22 The store rooms are below ground .... and are very cool
   and dark, especially in winter.
   A level B floor C depth D standard E height

23 We managed to grab a piece of wood that was floating
   nearby, and we hung on for .... life.
   A dear B kind C good D gentle E precious

24 Three stone .... lead up to the front door.
   A levels B stones C stairs D steps E rungs

25 Oh! You made me ....! I didn't hear you come in.
   A scream B jump C die D afraid E startle

26 It's not true that you haven't enough time for the work,
   Baxter. It's .... laziness.
   A rather B complete C altogether D sheer E full

27 Sweep the .... off the tablecloth, Gladys, before you
   put it away in the drawer.
   A dirt B crumbs C dust D rubbish E spots

28 Mr Ringer told the police that someone had broken down
   his garden fence, and the sergeant said they would ....
   the matter.
   A see over B watch over C find out D try over
   E look into

29 Stop ...., you two in the back row! You are adults, not
   school-girls!
   A smiling B joking C speaking D giggling
   E roaring

30 We tried to persuade Mother to buy a colour television set
   but she would not be ....
   A advised B influenced C assured D controlled
   E convinced

31 Bill Thomas is a most .... young man, and can do a lot
   of different jobs well.
   A industrious B diligent C laborious D capable
   E cunning

32 Let's have a cup of tea. Put the .... on, Polly.
   A hat B electricity C kettle D saucepan E tea-pot

33 Have you got a .... in your bag? It's so dark here that
   I can't even see the path.
   A torch B bulb C lamp D lantern E candle

34 Hearing a knock at the front door, Mrs Reed threw a ....
   over her pyjamas and went downstairs.
   A skirt B dressing-gown C scarf D nightdress
   E evening dress

35 The cupboard was quite close to the wall, but Paul, being
   thin, managed to .... behind it.
   A squeeze B crush C press D lower E flatten

36 Most .... birds are more brilliantly coloured than their
   wives.
   A he B masculine C male D master E husband

37 Five, seven, nine, eleven and thirteen are .... numbers.
   A large B unequal C prime D single E odd

38 That shop sells .... clothes, but they are usually quite
   well-made.
   A antique B ancient C old D old-fashioned
   E elderly

39 There were some .... flowers standing in a vase on the
   table.
   A imitation B artificial C false D forged E untrue

72

40 How much sugar would you like in your tea? Two ...., please.
   A lumps B parts C sections D squares E fragments

Section B

In this section you will find after each passage a number of questions or unfinished sentences, each with four suggested ways of finishing it. You must choose the one which you think fits best. Cross through the letter A, B, C or D for the answer you choose. Give one answer only to each question. Read each passage right through before choosing your answers.

First Passage

Dick May is a coal-miner. His young son, Stephen, has just passed an examination which will give him a scholarship to the local high school.

The next day, shortly after six o'clock, Stephen rushed home from Mr Cust's in a state of great excitement. To celebrate his success the vicar had given him a fountain pen.

'Look, Mum, isn't it a beauty!' he cried in ecstasy. He glanced at the table laid for tea, awaiting his father's return from the   5
pit. 'Where's Dad?' he asked.

'He's late,' replied Mrs May, looking at Stephen's pen. 'You certainly are a lucky boy.'

There was a tap at the back door. She went to it, and found there Fred Emmett and Henry Dyson, two miners who worked   10
with her husband. They were old friends of Dick's and at once Mrs May asked them in.

'He hasn't come back yet – but he'll be back any minute now. Do sit down,' she said.

They did not sit down, and it was then, in the light as they   15
entered the kitchen, that she saw that they had all the grime of the pit on them. Her heart gave a leap, but she said, quite calmly, as they stood awkwardly before her, 'What is it?'

'Mrs May, we've bad news for you,' said the elder man, Fred Emmett. 'It's about Dick.'   20

He hesitated and looked from Mrs May to his companion, as if hoping he would become the spokesman.

'There's been an accident?' asked Mrs May.

73

'No, not an accident. About ten minutes before we were
25 knocking off I was coming out of the gallery when I suddenly
found someone in a heap at my feet. I stooped down. It was
Dick. I couldn't get a word from him – he was on his face when
I found him – and I tried to lift him up, but he was so limp I put
him down again and called for the boys. It wasn't any use, Mrs
30 May, he'd gone. We brought him up, and the doctor looked
at him – he was dead. He must have just dropped – gone in a
second, the doctor said. So they've taken him to the mortuary,
and we've come . . .'
      'The mortuary – why haven't you brought him home?'
35 demanded Mrs May, her face white and strained.
      'He has to go to the mortuary – there'll be an inquest. Seems
it has to be done that way. That's the law, Mrs May. The
Manager asked us to come and tell you – you'll be wanting to
go and see him? We're terribly sorry, Mrs May. We all liked
40 Dick. And he never seemed ill, he got tired like – we all do, and
get over it.'
      'They want me now? Can you go with me?'
      'Of course. Someone had to come and tell you.'
      'It's kind of you. Then there wasn't an accident, an explosion?
45 No one was killed – I'm glad of that.'
      'No.'
      'I'll get my hat. Won't you sit down a minute?' she said, and
as Stephen rushed to her, in tears, she put her hand on his head,
saying gently, 'If you come with me, you must be brave.'
50 Stephen nodded, as he pressed against her. She released him,
went upstairs, and soon returned, ready for the street. She
picked up Stephen's school cap and put it on his head. Then she
stirred the fire and added some coal.
      'Let us go,' she said, turning to the two miners awkwardly
55 standing before her, their caps in their hands. 'I hope I shan't
do anything silly, like fainting.'
      She took Stephen's hand and led the way out of the room.

41 Mrs May
    A   was expecting Fred Emmett and Henry Dyson to call.
    B   was waiting for her husband to come home from work.
    C   did not know Fred Emmett and Henry Dyson.
    D   thought that Fred Emmett and Henry Dyson had
        brought her husband home.

42 Why did the two men come to the Mays' house?
   A To bring home Dick May's body.
   B To ask Mrs May if her husband had died.
   C To tell Mrs May not to go to the mortuary.
   D To tell Mrs May that her husband was dead.

43 The first indication that Mrs May had that the two men
   had brought bad news was when
   A they did not sit down.
   B she saw that they had not washed.
   C they tapped on the back door.
   D they said 'Mrs May, we've bad news for you.'

44 Dick May died
   A of a heart attack.
   B following a fall.
   C quite suddenly.
   D of over-work.

45 Dick May was taken to the mortuary because
   A an inquiry had to be made.
   B all people who died in the mine had to be taken there.
   C he had not died in an accident.
   D the doctor was not sure why he had died.

46 The two men said that
   A Mr May had been very tired before he died.
   B all the men in the mine were tired and ill.
   C they had thought he would get over his illness.
   D they did not know that he was ill.

47 Mrs May was glad that
   A the men had come to tell her.
   B that there had been no accident.
   C her husband had not suffered.
   D her husband had been taken to the mortuary.

48 Stephen
   A˙ was not brave enough to go to the mortuary with his
     mother.
   B had to go to the mortuary with his mother.
   C promised his mother that he would be brave.
   D didn't understand what the two miners had said to his
     mother.

49 How did Mrs May receive the news of her husband's death?
    A   Bravely and calmly.
    B   She nearly fainted.
    C   Without any emotion.
    D   As if she didn't care.

50 Mrs May went upstairs
    A   because she was very upset.
    B   to get Stephen's school cap.
    C   to put on her coat and hat.
    D   because she wanted to be alone.

Second Passage

It is not every day that one gets the opportunity to go round the
world – especially at the age of sixty-nine – and Gladys, who
was getting rather bored with doing nothing in particular in
her tiny flat at the seaside, didn't think twice. She read the
5   letter through, made herself a cup of tea, and then put her
glasses on and read the letter through again to make sure that
she had not misunderstood what Mrs Ablewhite was
suggesting.

    Then she sat down and wrote a short letter, saying that she
10 could be ready to leave at practically any time, and that she
would see about having the necessary inoculations immediately. She signed her name at the bottom, put the letter in an
envelope, drank another cup of tea, and then went along to the
post-box on the corner. She wanted to be quite sure that her
15 reply arrived as quickly as possible; after all – who knows? –
Mrs Ablewhite might have other acquaintances who would
jump as eagerly at the chance of accompanying a lonely rich
woman on a world cruise.

    It was Friday, and Bernard called in on his way home from
20 work as he always did. He was full of chat as usual and as he
went on about Bobbie's school report, and Carol's hair (which
she had had dyed red but the result was far too vivid for their
liking) and the arrival of Paul's third tooth, Gladys' thoughts
wandered to Gibraltar, Colombo, Singapore, Hawaii (would
25 they touch Hawaii, she wondered?) San Francisco . . .

    'Uh?' She was aware that Bernard had asked her something,
and, for once in a while, was waiting for an answer. 'What did
you say, dear?'

'Aunt Gladys, you haven't heard a word I've been saying! And I can't stop and tell you all over again because I promised Carol I'd be home by seven because she's got a meeting that she specially wants to go to tonight, and the girl from next door – you know, Sarah Butler, that tall red-haired girl with glasses – can't come in and baby-sit as she usually does. I just wanted to tell you that Carol says that when you come at Christmas would you mind just this once sharing a room with her cousin Maude? I think you met Maude once – yes, it was at Paul's christening. Do you remember? She's about forty and looks rather like a horse . . .' 30 35

'Yes, I remember her very well. I liked her,' said Gladys. 'Of course I would be quite happy to share a room with her. But there's no need . . .' 40

'That's all right, then. I'll tell Carol she needn't worry. She has been rather concerned about where everyone is going to sleep. We shall be quite a house-full this year, you see. Mother's coming of course, and then Pam and Alan said they'd bring Sue and Frank over to see us – they'll be home from Canada – but they'll only stay for lunch on Christmas Day, I expect, and then there's old Mr Foley and his sister who always . . .' 45

'Bernard, listen to me for just a moment,' interrupted Gladys, firmly. 'Tell Carol there's no need to worry about where I'm going to sleep at Christmas because I shan't be here.' 50

'What do you mean?' Bernard's long and rather stupid face looked worried. 'Oh, Auntie, you never said! I never realized you were ill! Oh, I am so sorry . . .' 55

'I'm not going to die, you idiot,' retorted Gladys. 'I never felt better in my life. No, I'm going on a world cruise.'

'You're going on a WHAT?' yelled Bernard after a moment's incredulous silence.

'A world cruise,' repeated Gladys, studying her nails, 'with Mrs Ablewhite. We leave some time in November from Southampton. I don't know exactly when we get back, but I do know that we shall be spending Christmas in Sydney.' 60

51 When Gladys received an invitation to go round the world
   A   she did not understand immediately.
   B   she was drinking a cup of tea.
   C   she accepted at once.
   D   she thought she was too old to go.

52 Mrs Ablewhite was
  A a close friend of Gladys'.
  B one of Gladys' relations.
  C Gladys' former employer.
  D rich and lonely.

53 When Bernard called, Gladys
  A was too excited to listen to his family news.
  B asked about his wife and children.
  C wandered about but didn't listen to him.
  D was bored by his conversation.

54 What do you know about Carol's hair?
  A She had dyed it red.
  B Bernard had dyed it red for her.
  C Carol and Bernard thought it was not red enough.
  D It had been dyed bright red.

55 Gladys
  A had been invited to spend Christmas with Bernard
     and Carol.
  B didn't usually spend Christmas with her nephew and
     his wife.
  C shared a room with Carol's cousin Maude at
     Christmas.
  D usually spent Christmas in her little flat at the seaside.

56 Bernard could not repeat his news because
  A he was in a hurry to get home.
  B his wife's hair was being dyed red.
  C the baby-sitter had not arrived.
  D it was past seven o'clock.

57 Why was it difficult for Gladys to tell Bernard about her
    cruise?
  A She thought that he might be disappointed that she
     was going away.
  B Bernard and Carol had already made their plans for
     Christmas.
  C Bernard talked so much that it was hard for her to say
     anything.
  D Bernard wanted her to share her room with Carol's
     cousin Maude.

58 When Gladys said 'I shan't be here' (line 52), Bernard
    A   was worried about where she was going to sleep.
    B   thought that she was not telling the truth.
    C   didn't understand what she was trying to say.
    D   wanted to know where she was going for Christmas.

59 When Bernard heard that Gladys was going on a world
    cruise
    A   he was very disappointed and shocked.
    B   he thought she was going to die.
    C   he could hardly believe his ears.
    D   he was angry and shouted at her.

60 The conversation between Gladys and Bernard took place
    A   in November.
    B   a few days before Christmas.
    C   in Southampton.
    D   in Gladys' home.

Test Paper 8

Section A

In this section you must choose the word or phrase which best completes each sentence. Cross through the letter A, B, C, D or E for the word or phrase you choose. Give one answer only for each question.

1   You should never listen to Miss Perkins; half of what she says is just silly ....
    A speech   **B** words   **C** stories   **D** gossip   **E** chat

2   Pensions are given to people who lose .... in industrial accidents.
    A legs   **B** arms   **C** heads   **D** pieces   **E** limbs

3   We packed most of our books in strong .... boxes.
    A paper   **B** cardboard   **C** carton   **D** wrapping   **E** brown

4   Aunt Clara is coming to dinner? Oh dear! It will be very .... explaining to her why we aren't using that horrible tablecloth she sent us last Christmas.
    A ashamed   **B** awkward   **C** impossible   **D** offended
    E dangerous

5   Uncle Barney was a man of great .... ; unfortunately, he didn't leave any of it to me.
    A wealth   **B** money   **C** richness   **D** gold   **E** cash

6   Keep ....! Don't panic! You will soon be rescued!
    A down   **B** happy   **C** brave   **D** cool   **E** firm

7   He .... down and picked up the glove that she had dropped on the pavement.
    A lay   **B** curved   **C** bent   **D** stood   **E** turned

8　You are not very .... today, Sam. What's the matter?
　　I've never known you so quiet.
　　A loud　**B** talkative　**C** speaking　**D** chattering
　　E conversational

9　Mummy! Mummy! My beautiful big blue balloon has
　　.........!
　　A broken　**B** exploded　**C** crashed　**D** fallen　**E** burst

10　If you think that I am going to lend you any more money,
　　you are very much ....
　　A mistaken　**B** wrong　**C** disappointed　**D** out
　　E misunderstood

11　The butcher's shop was an old-fashioned one and there was
　　......... on the floor.
　　A powder　**B** wood　**C** soil　**D** sawdust　**E** stones

12　The .... of the *Rose Marie* is only a few yards from the
　　beach, and we swam out to it yesterday.
　　A remains　**B** last　**C** rest　**D** ruin　**E** wreck

13　Mother cannot bear to see anyone ...., and she is always
　　finding little jobs for us to do.
　　A still　**B** workless　**C** idle　**D** restful　**E** staying

14　The harbour is too .... for any very large ships to come
　　in.
　　A deep　**B** low　**C** wet　**D** shallow　**E** dry

15　We wandered .... about the garden, wondering how to
　　pass the time.
　　A quickly　**B** stupidly　**C** aimlessly　**D** hopefully
　　E dirtily

16　I stood between two .... women on the crowded bus,
　　and I could hardly breathe.
　　A great　**B** famous　**C** slight　**D** huge　**E** wide

17　I dropped a heavy box on my foot and broke one of my
　　..........
　　A bones　**B** fingers　**C** toes　**D** pieces　**E** knuckles

18 The epidemic seems to be dying out; only three .... of cholera were reported last week.
A pieces B illnesses C diseases D cases
E emergencies

19 I must buy a new dress; I am going to a .... on Friday.
A marriage B matrimony C feast D wedding
E bride

20 Bill Foster was very angry when a man insulted his wife, and he .... him on the nose.
A punched B boxed C stroked D pushed E smacked

21 That medicine was horrible! Give me a piece of chocolate to take the .... away.
A smell B sensation C feeling D taste E bitter

22 She .... gently on the door, and said 'May I come in, please?'
A beat B hammered C hit D tapped E pushed

23 I saw Aunt Phyllis on the other side of the road, so I .... to attract her attention.
A spoke B moved C threw D blinked E waved

24 Gerald Blake lives in a large .... of flats near Regent's Park.
A house B block C palace D building E case

25 His bedroom .... the park.
A undertakes B overtakes C undergoes D overlooks
E oversees

26 Cousin Bella usually wears a hat to keep her hair ....
A on B up C well D pretty E tidy

27 The child is .... with sitting indoors; let him go and play in the garden.
A bored B tired C dull D sad E angry

28 I'm afraid your luggage is five kilos ....; you will have to pay extra.
A overmuch B excess C overweight D heavy
E above

29 You will recognize my grandfather by his long white
....
A face B trousers C legs D nose E beard

30 I can't .... the time at the moment; can you come back
the day after tomorrow?
A give B spare C offer D make E get

31 After considering the ...., the jury decided that the man
was not guilty.
A evidence B story C proof D summons E crime

32 Jane .... into tears and rushed out of the room sobbing.
A fell B broke C came D burst E cried

33 They say that this house is ...., but I have lived here for
six years and I have never seen a ghost.
A dangerous B enchanted C cursed D haunted
E superstitious

34 What a .... colour that wallpaper is! Why ever did you
buy it?
A bad B naughty C wicked D frightening E nasty

35 'What are your neighbours like?' 'Well, I'm afraid I don't
.... with them very well.'
A come in B go out C see to D get on E sit down

36 I've got his name on the tip of my .... Whatever is he
called? I'll remember it in just a minute!
A nose B tongue C head D brain E thought

37 We shall have to .... a new contract and then ask you to
sign it.
A pull out B write down C think of D draw up
E get in

38 I'm sorry, Madam, we are out of .... of Glu-Glu-Glu
toothpaste until next week.
A supplies B tubes C touch D hand E stock

39 Religious intolerance is much less .... than it used to
be a hundred years ago.
A hard B popular C widespread D universal
E planned

40 I want to propose Mr Jackson as Chairman. Will you
.... it?
A support B second C bear D agree E vote

Section B

*In this section you will find after each passage a number of
questions or unfinished statements, each with four suggested
ways of finishing it. You must choose the one which you think
fits best. Cross through the letter A, B, C or D for the answer you
choose. Give one answer only to each question. Read each passage
right through before choosing your answers.*

First Passage

A shot smashed the wing-mirror and I trod on the accelerator
even harder, trying to coax a little more speed out of the
screaming engine. Beside me Pat was quite calm, but I could
sense that she was as terrified as I was. She was clinging on to
5   her seat so as not to be thrown on to me as we hurtled round
bends and corners, and bounced up and down on the rough
surface. It was no more than a cart track, really. My only
thought was to get to a town or village or at least to some sign
of humanity – they would never dare shoot us down in cold
10 blood in front of witnesses. At least, I hoped they wouldn't.
The little van was out of sight now round one of the bends,
but when we came to an unexpectedly straight part of the lane
I could see it behind us in the driving-mirror. With one eye on
the road ahead and the other on the van behind, I saw Carter
15 lean out of the window and point a gun at us. Then there was a
crash as our rear window exploded, a bullet whistled between
our heads, and the windscreen shattered into a thick white fog.
'Knock it out, Pat! For God's sake, knock it out!' I screamed.
Pat was sobbing, choking back her fear, and with her gloved
20 hands she beat at the windscreen, using her handbag as a
hammer, and managed to knock a hole through which I could
see the road ahead. The wind blew the broken glass in and my
lap and chest were covered with little pebbles of glass. Now an

84

icy gale whistled through the hole and made it difficult for me
to see where we were going. My eyes were watering and it was   25
all I could do to make out the bends in the lane. The gathering
dusk didn't make things any easier, either.

By this time Pat had knocked out the broken windscreen
on her side too.

'I think there's a main road ahead, Dan,' she said, quite   30
quietly. Her glasses protected her eyes and they were watering
less than mine. 'I can see a lot of traffic through those trees over
there.'

Another shot passed uncomfortably close to my ear as I
managed to force the speedometer up another fraction of an   35
inch.

'Oh please God let me make it – let me make it,' I whispered.

Then, sure enough, there was a sign by the side of the road –
GIVE WAY – and I could see a steady stream of traffic in the
main road we were about to join. I didn't give way. I just shot   40
straight out and we were lucky not to get hit by one of the many
drivers who registered their protest by hooting at us angrily.
Better to get hurt in a road accident than to be shot down like
a rabbit, I thought, very selfishly. Pat was looking back over
her shoulder.   45

'They've gone, Dan,' she said, softly. 'Oh darling, they've
gone,' and she started to cry with relief.

Sure enough, they must have stayed in the lane, for there
was no sign of the van in the driving-mirror now.

'What now?' Pat asked after a few moments.   50

'The first thing is to get to a telephone box,' I said, 'and in
any case we can't drive very far like this. We'll freeze to death.
Look, there's a big garage in front on the left. We can phone
from there and we shall be safe – at any rate for the time being.
And we can probably get the windscreen replaced.'   55

When we pulled into the garage forecourt a few seconds later
we were both glad to see that there was a little café there, with
welcoming, bright, warm, steamy windows. It was crowded.
You can feel safe in a crowd.

41 It was a difficult drive because
    A   the lane was only a cart track.
    B   their car wouldn't go very fast.
    C   the lane was twisty and rough.
    D   the driver of the car had been shot.

42 Dan thought that
   A   Carter and his associates wanted to break their windscreen.
   B   Carter would not kill them unless he could do it unobserved.
   C   they could escape from Carter because their car was faster.
   D   Carter and his associates did not really intend to kill them.

43 Why did Pat have to knock out the broken windscreen?
   A   Because the people behind were shooting at them.
   B   Because Dan could not see to drive.
   C   Because wind was blowing through the hole.
   D   Because the rear window had exploded.

44 Dan couldn't see very well because
   A   it was dark.
   B   his eyes were watering.
   C   the windscreen was broken.
   D   he was afraid.

45 Pat could see better than Dan because
   A   she was not driving.
   B   the windscreen was not broken on her side.
   C   she was wearing glasses.
   D   she had better eyesight.

46 After the third shot, Dan
   A   saw some traffic.
   B   went a little faster.
   C   could not see the road.
   D   reached a main road.

47 What did Dan and Pat do when they reached the main road?
   A   They had a road accident.
   B   They hooted at the other cars.
   C   They shot at the traffic.
   D   They disobeyed the sign.

48 Why does the writer use the word 'selfishly' (line 44)?
   A Because Dan was not thinking of Pat.
   B Because the people in the van might have got hurt too.
   C Because Dan was not considering other drivers.
   D Because he did not want to shoot rabbits.

49 Carter and his associates
   A could not catch Dan and Pat on the main road.
   B had to stay in the lane.
   C were not able to drive on to the main road.
   D decided not to follow Dan on to the main road.

50 They thought they would be safe at the garage
   A because it was a very cold evening.
   B and that they could continue the journey later.
   C because the café was crowded and warm.
   D and that the garage would be warm and crowded.

Second Passage

When Sir Edward Travers died suddenly and mysteriously,
there was consternation and speculation throughout the
country. A paragraph in our local paper stated:
   'With the death of Sir Edward Travers, the eminent archaeo-   5
logist, who recently left this country to carry out excavations
among the tombs of the Pharaohs, it is being asked: Is there
any truth in the ancient belief that he who meddles with the
resting places of the dead invites their enmity? Sir Edward's
sudden death has brought the expedition to an abrupt end.'
   Sir Ralph Bodrean, our local Squire and Sir Edward's closest   10
friend, had given financial aid to the expedition, and when a
few days after the announcement of Sir Edward's death, Sir
Ralph had a stroke, there was further speculation that these
misfortunes were the result of the Curse of the Kings.
   Sir Edward's body was brought back and buried in our   15
churchyard, and Tybalt, Sir Edward's only son, who had already attained some distinction in the same profession as his
father, was, of course, chief mourner.
   At the funeral I could not take my eyes from Tybalt. I had
loved him, hopelessly, from the time I had first seen him, but   20

what chance had I with such a man? He was by no means handsome but he was distinguished looking – very tall and lean. He had the brow of a scholar, yet there was a touch of sensuality about his mouth and his grey eyes were deep-set and veiled. One could never be quite certain what he was thinking.

A few days after the funeral my footsteps led me to Giza House, the home of the Travers family. Now that the funeral was over and the blinds had been drawn up, it no longer looked melancholy. It had regained that air of mystery with which I had always associated it. To my embarrassment Tybalt came out of the house.

'Good afternoon, Miss Osmond,' he said. 'You must come in.' He smiled at me which made me feel ridiculously happy. It was absurd for down-to-earth Miss Osmond to feel so intensely about another human being!

Tybald took me into the drawing-room and signed to me to sit down. 'We're planning another expedition to the place where my father died,' he said.

I did not believe in this story of the curse, yet the thought of his going back there alarmed me. 'You think that wise?' I asked.

'Surely you don't believe these rumours about my father's death, do you, Miss Osmond?'

'Of course not.'

'He was a healthy man, it is true. And suddenly he was struck down when he was on the verge of a great discovery. The day before he died he said: "I believe shortly I am going to prove to everyone that this expedition was very much worthwhile." He would say no more than that. How I wish he had!' Tybald winked regretfully.

'There was an autopsy?'

'Yes, but they were unable to find the cause. And now Sir Ralph . . .'

'You don't think there is a connection?'

He shook his head. 'I think Sir Ralph was shocked by his old friend's sudden death. Sir Ralph had a mild stroke once before, and his doctors have been warning him for years to show a little moderation. No, Sir Ralph's illness has nothing to do with Egypt. Well, I am going back to find out what it was my father was on the point of discovering.'

'When will you leave?'

'In three months.'

51 Everyone talked about the death of Sir Edward Travers because
    A   he was a famous archaeologist.
    B   there was something strange about it.
    C   he had been carrying out excavations.
    D   the expedition had unexpectedly ended.

52 Where did Sir Edward Travers die?
    A   In the country.
    B   At Giza House.
    C   We do not know.
    D   In Egypt.

53 What was the Curse of the Kings?
    A   That anyone who tried to find the tombs of the Pharaohs would die mysteriously.
    B   That Sir Edward Travers and Sir Ralph Bodrean would die suddenly and in mysterious circumstances.
    C   That whoever meddled with a tomb would have a great many enemies.
    D   That misfortune would come to whoever interfered with the Pharaohs' burial places.

54 Tybalt Travers was
    A   in love with Miss Osmond.
    B   tall, dark and handsome.
    C   a distinguished archaeologist.
    D   mysterious and mournful.

55 Why did Miss Osmond go to Giza House a few days after the funeral?
    A   Because she hoped she might meet Tybalt.
    B   She went completely by chance.
    C   To visit the Travers family.
    D   To find out about the new expedition.

56 Why was it absurd for Miss Osmond to feel so ridiculously happy?
    A   Because she was usually a realistic person with no romantic ideas.
    B   Because she was very upset and sad about the death of Sir Edward Travers.

C Because although she was in love with Tybalt she knew he wouldn't marry her.

D Because she was very poor and had little reason to feel happy.

57 Miss Osmond was rather unhappy to hear that Tybalt was going to Egypt
    A although she was not superstitious.
    B because she was a very wise girl.
    C because she did not want him to leave her.
    D and tried to persuade him not to go.

58 Sir Edward Travers died
    A after a short illness which was quite unexpected.
    B before Tybalt could discover what his secret was.
    C and could not tell anyone what he hoped to discover.
    D of a stroke, after discovering something important.

59 Was Sir Ralph's illness very sudden?
    A No – he had been ill for years.
    B Yes – but it was not unexpected.
    C Yes – he had been quite well until then.
    D No – he used to have strokes quite regularly.

60 Why did Tybalt want to go to Egypt?
    A To discover what his father had not.
    B To find out why his father had died.
    C To see the tombs of the Pharaohs.
    D To avenge his father's death.

Test Paper 9

Section A

In this section you must choose the word or phrase which best completes each sentence. Cross through the letter A, B, C, D or E for the word or phrase you choose. Give one answer only for each question.

1 The aeroplane crashed into the hillside and .... into flames.
    A turned **B** exploded **C** came **D** got **E** burst

2 What .... weather! I don't feel like going out.
    A sad **B** grey **C** miserable **D** poor **E** heavy

3 She was filled with .... at the news of her brother's death.
    A agitation **B** grief **C** pain **D** anxiety **E** tears

4 Cars can drive through the centre of the town, but lorries are advised to take the ....
    A flyover **B** roundabout **C** underground **D** bypass
    E outlet

5 Her uncle has a big .... store in one of the industrial towns in the north.
    A dresses **B** garments **C** wearing **D** suits **E** clothing

6 Stop ...., Sylvia! Haven't you got a handkerchief?
    A blowing **B** running **C** coughing **D** sniffing
    E smelling

7 Uncle Reginald .... so loudly all night long that I couldn't sleep at all.
    A slept **B** woke **C** yawned **D** snored **E** grunted

8   As James opened the door, the candle .... in the breeze
    and then went out.
    A flickered   B shone   C sparkled   D twinkled
    E flamed

9   She was in a dark red velvet dress, with a diamond ....
    at her throat.
    A rope   B string   C collar   D bracelet   E necklace

10 There was a sudden .... of lightning, followed by a loud
    roar of thunder.
    A stroke   B lamp   C spark   D crash   E flash

11 I'm a doctor, not a magician. I can't .... miracles, you
    know.
    A make   B work   C get   D set   E do

12 There was a sharp .... and the plate broke into two
    pieces.
    A bang   B crash   C roar   D noise   E crack

13 The exact cause of the disaster is not yet known, but the
    authorities think that some dry grass may have ....
    fire.
    A taken   B got   C made   D caught   E lighted

14 My boss .... quite mad when he heard what I had done.
    A made   B took   C got   D became   E went

15 We shall have to use that cup as we are a glass ....
    A less   B few   C minus   D under   E short

16 What they say may be true; you never can ....
    A know   B say   C tell   D remember   E recognize

17 I was in the High Street last week when a woman was
    knocked down by a car, and now I have been summoned to
    appear in court as a ....
    A witness   B prisoner   C observer   D evidence
    E testimony

18 An old gypsy came to the door this morning and offered
to tell my ....
A luck B fortune C life D future E destiny

19 Give me a packet of needles and a .... of black cotton,
please.
A roll B reel C bundle D pound E yard

20 It was such a still day that not a .... of grass was moving
in the meadow.
A blade B piece C leaf D bit E stalk

21 I did my best to arrive on time but the heavy traffic ....
me.
A blocked B held C hindered D kept E pulled

22 So you fell and hurt yourself! Well, it .... you right!
I told you not to climb up on to that wall.
A does B gives C makes D gets E serves

23 Put the .... back on the biscuit tin, otherwise the
biscuits will go soft.
A lid B top C cover D cap E fastener

24 This road will be closed to traffic until further ....
A advice B notice C news D indication
E movement

25 Did they tell you to get dinner ready? No, I did it of my
own ....
A will B accord C want D idea E desire

26 A strange flag was .... from the top of the tower.
A showing B making C going D flying E blowing

27 'I've brought you a cup of tea, Aunt Helen.' 'Thank you,
dear. That is .... of you.'
A thoughtful B hopeful C gentle D sympathetic
E brave

28 Go straight along the road, and keep left where it ....
after the cemetery.
A divides B parts C forks D splits E doubles

29 Don't .... to knock; walk straight in.
A think B wait C hesitate D try E bother

30 After dinner, we went for a quiet .... along the beach in
the moonlight.
A rush B wander C sit D stroll E play

31 We were quite .... by the fantastic welcome we were
given at the airport.
A shocked B conquered C overwhelmed D beaten
E done in

32 Yes, that coat is just the colour I have been looking for.
May I ...., please?
A put it on B try it on C wear it D fit it E prove it

33 Uncle Charles has a farm in Yorkshire, where he ....
horses.
A makes B multiplies C breeds D raises E runs

34 Fighting has .... in several parts of the country.
A gone in B set up C broken out D got down
E come on

35 I think it would be very .... to take a decision at this
moment.
A crazy B not advised C unwise D hopeless
E bad mannered

36 Your shoes are a ...., Peter! You haven't cleaned them
for weeks.
A disgrace B shock C blow D accident E shame

37 It was a great .... to go up in a helicopter for the first
time.
A like B rise C incident D thrill E suspense

38 .... Emma getting married at last! Everyone thought
she was going to be an old maid.
A like B so C think D fancy E wonder

39 'Have all these letters typed in triplicate, Miss Jones.'
'Certainly, Mr Moneybags. I'll .... it at once.'
A do for   B think of   C make for   D see to   E get on

40 I could tell that Jean was frightened because she .... my
arm hard.
A pulled   B stretched   C heaved   D bruised   E gripped

Section B

*In this section you will find after each passage a number of
questions or unfinished statements, each with four suggested
ways of finishing it. You must choose the one which you think
fits best. Cross through the letter A, B, C or D for the answer you
choose. Give one answer only to each question. Read each
passage right through before choosing your answers.*

First Passage

*Richard Hillary is in Scotland, training to be a pilot, at the
beginning of the Second World War.*

Many times of an evening I would stand on the shore and
look out to sea, where a curious phosphorescent green was
changing to a transparent blue. Behind the camp the setting
sun, like a flaming ball, painted the mountains purple and gold.
The air was like champagne, and as we were in the Gulf Stream   5
the weather was beautifully mild. While violent snowstorms
were raging in England, we were enjoying the most perfect
flying weather and a day which lasted for nearly twenty-four
hours.
  On leave for four days, Noel and I drove across Scotland to   10
the west coast and took the ferry over to Skye. The small stone
quay was spotted with shops; a bus was drawn up by the water-
side, a hotel advertisement on its side. I looked at Noel and he
nodded. We had come prepared to be disappointed. But we had
not driven far before the road gave way to a winding track and   15
the only signs of habitation were a few crofters' cottages. It
was evening when we drew up outside the Sligachan Inn at the
foot of the Coolin Mountains. The innkeeper welcomed us and
showed us our rooms.
  From every window was the same view, grey mountains   20

rising in austere beauty, their peaks hidden in a white mist, and everywhere a great feeling of stillness. The shadows that lengthened across the valley, the streams that coursed down the rocks, the thin mist turning now into night, all a part of that stillness. I shivered; Skye was a world that one would either love or hate. There could be no in-between.

'It is very beautiful,' said the landlord.

'Yes,' I said, 'it's beautiful.'

'But only mountaineers or fools will climb those peaks.'

'We're both fools,' Noel said shortly.

'So be it. Dinner is at eight-thirty.'

We stood a while at the window. The night was clear and our heads felt clear and cold as the air. We smelled the odour of the ground in the spring after rain, and behind us the wood smoke of the pine fire in our room, and we were content. For these are the odours of nostalgia, spring mist and wood smoke, and never the scent of a woman or of food.

We were alone in the inn save for one old man who had returned there to die. His hair was white, but his face and bearing were still those of a mountaineer, though he must have been a great age. He never spoke, but appeared regularly at meals to take his place at a table tight-pressed against the window, alone with his wine and his memories. We thought him rather fine.

41 The camp was
   A   in the Gulf Stream.
   B   on the beach.
   C   between the mountains and the sea.
   D   between Scotland and England.

42 At the time of this episode
   A   it was very warm in Scotland.
   B   days were longer in Scotland than in England.
   C   the weather was good all over Britain.
   D   it was good weather for flying in England.

43 How was it possible for Hillary and Noel to go to Skye?
   A   They had finished their flying training.
   B   The weather was not good for flying.
   C   They had a short holiday.
   D   They needed a rest after training.

44 Noel and the writer
    A did not expect to like Skye very much.
    B knew Skye well.
    C thought that Skye would be very lonely.
    D were looking for a particular hotel on Skye.

45 How did they reach the Sligachan Inn?
    A By ferry.
    B On foot.
    C By car.
    D We do not know.

46 When Noel said 'We're both fools' (line 30) what did he
    mean?
    A 'We don't know anything about climbing mountains.'
    B 'We think that those peaks are too difficult for us to
       climb.'
    C 'We are angry that you have suggested that we might
       be fools.'
    D 'We are going to climb, although we are not expert
       climbers.'

47 They liked the Sligachan Inn because
    A the landlord was friendly and the food was good.
    B there were fine views and it was very quiet.
    C it was in a valley near the foot of the mountains.
    D it was better than the hotels near the quay.

48 During their stay on Skye
    A they were alone in the inn.
    B they were cold.
    C they intended to climb mountains.
    D they ate at 8.30 every evening.

49 The old man in the hotel
    A was very ill and likely to die soon.
    B wanted to die near the mountains.
    C was unfriendly and refused to speak.
    D had been a famous mountaineer.

50 How did Hillary know that the old man had been a moun-
    taineer?

A Because the landlord told him so.
B By the way he walked and looked.
C Because he was a silent man.
D He didn't know – he guessed.

Second Passage

Although it was well past midnight, there were plenty of folk about. A group of expensively-dressed people were chatting at the entrance to platform four, and, when I glanced at the indicator and saw that a train from Bristol was due to arrive
5 there in a few minutes, I imagined that they were meeting someone off it. They were. The train came in and disgorged its load. A rather theatrical-looking young woman came lurching along the platform on the thickest of thick soles and the highest of high chunky heels, and cried: 'Mummy! Daddy! How sweet
10 of you to come! And Auntie May! And darling, darling . . .' I didn't catch the name of the particular darling in question as the shrill voice was by now muffled in the furs of its various female relations. After a few seconds, during which it seemed that everyone kissed everyone else, they moved off in a group,
15 with much hand waving and loud laughter, everybody talking at once and nobody listening at all.

Two sailors, (waiting for the last train to Portsmouth, I supposed), viewed them from the bench they were sitting on. One was eyeing the theatrical-looking young lady with what
20 could only be called a lustful eye. Had she not been surrounded by her nearest and dearest he would have tried his luck, it was clear. The other, a somewhat older fellow, was cynically smiling at the extrovert antics of the family in general. I guessed he was comparing them with his own family at home.
25 A woman of indefinite age and shape, muffled up in what appeared to be two coats, several hats, and innumerable scarves, was sitting on the bench under the clock, eating digestive biscuits out of a paper bag and talking to herself. She was surrounded by plastic carrier-bags, each one filled to
30 bursting. I imagined that these were her only possessions, and that the bench she was sitting on was the only place that she could accurately call home. Such people are not uncommon in large cities, and they always seem to gravitate to the main railway station – perhaps it is the warmest place at night.
35 I was so intent on watching the panorama of life around me

that I had not noticed a man sit down on the bench beside me.
In fact, it was not until he was very close indeed – so close that
by reaching out he could put a hand on my knee – that I even
realized he was there. And when he did just that, I jumped and
gave a little scream – not because I am the sort of girl that   40
behaves in that way generally but because I was honestly
startled.

He withdrew his hand quickly, but didn't move away. He
didn't say anything either, and he didn't even look at me. He
seemed to freeze inside.   45

I contemplated saying 'How dare you!' or 'Do you mind!' or
'Go away!', but discarded the first as too Victorian, the second
as too common and the third as too naïve. By then, of course,
it was too late to say anything at all. I got up and wandered to
the bookstall as if nothing had happened.   50

51 The writer thought that the expensively-dressed people
    A were going to Bristol by train.
    B were talking far too much.
    C were waiting for someone to arrive.
    D were theatrical people.

52 'They were' (line 6) means
    A they were going to Bristol.
    B they were expensively dressed.
    C they were chatting at the entrance.
    D they were waiting for someone.

53 The theatrical-looking young woman walked strangely
    because
    A she was drunk.
    B she was an actress.
    C she was wearing fashionable shoes.
    D the platform was rough and uneven.

54 Why didn't the writer hear the name of 'darling' (line 11)?
    A The group of people had moved away.
    B The women were kissing the young lady.
    C The young woman's relations kept her quiet.
    D All the other people were talking loudly.

55 The younger sailor
    A tried to attract the attention of the young woman.
    B would have liked to invite the young woman for a
       drink.
    C wished that the young woman had been alone.
    D was shocked by the behaviour of the young woman's
       family.

56 The older sailor
    A found the young woman's family amusing.
    B disapproved of the way the family behaved.
    C wanted to be at home with his own family.
    D wished that his family were more fashionable.

57 The writer thought that the woman (line 25)
    A was homeless.
    B was not uncommon.
    C was in the station because it was warm.
    D had too many plastic carrier-bags.

58 Why didn't the writer notice the man sit down next to her?
    A He was a very insignificant sort of person.
    B She was too busy doing something else.
    C He arrived very quietly and secretly.
    D He didn't want her to notice that he was there.

59 What did the man do when the writer screamed?
    A He said nothing.
    B He looked away.
    C He ran away.
    D He froze.

60 Why did the writer say nothing to the man?
    A She was too angry to speak.
    B She didn't know what to say.
    C She didn't want to appear Victorian.
    D She thought it would be common to speak to him.

Test Paper 10

Section A

In this section you must choose the word or phrase which best completes each sentence. Cross through the letter A, B, C, D or E for the word or phrase you choose. Give one answer only for each question.

1   Ethel is a nice girl but she has one great ....; she talks too much.
    A sin   **B** failing   **C** mistake   **D** miss   **E** crime

2   No, these shoes .... my toes. Let me try a larger size, please.
    A hold   **B** grip   **C** compress   **D** break   **E** pinch

3   The .... at half-time was: Wanderers 2 – Rovers 0.
    A result   **B** number   **C** goals   **D** figure   **E** score

4   I used to be quite a .... smoker, but I gave it up several years ago.
    A heavy   **B** bad   **C** strong   **D** frequent   **E** lot

5   Please don't .... in front of the children, John. I don't want them to learn such words.
    A speak   **B** exclaim   **C** swear   **D** protest   **E** shout

6   I .... you can't tell me how many children Shakespeare had.
    A hope   **B** know   **C** suppose   **D** guess   **E** bet

7   Don't try to .... nuts with your teeth, Bill! You'll hurt yourself.
    A eat   **B** break   **C** chew   **D** crack   **E** open

D

8   You mustn't tell Aunt Grace that joke; she's very ....
    A broad-minded   B small-minded   C open-minded
    D narrow-minded   E simple-minded

9   The boxer in the dark .... is sure to win. He's much
    better than the other one.
    A pants   B trousers   C trunks   D slip   E costume

10 I must have these shoes repaired; there are big holes in
    the ....
    A bottoms   B soles   C floors   D underneath   E leather

11 When we go fishing we always take a lot of worms for
    ....
    A bait   B trap   C food   D attraction   E eating

12 The piano is badly out of ...., I'm afraid.
    A practice   B touch   C use   D tune   E melody.

13 That vase is Chinese, and is about 600 years old. It is ....,
    of course.
    A valueless   B priceless   C costly   D invalid
    E expensive

14 We hope to bring you further news of this in our next
    .... at nine o'clock.
    A instalment   B bulletin   C episode   D piece
    E article

15 'Well, I never!' .... Mrs Parsons. 'I can hardly believe
    my eyes!'
    A asked   B shouted   C wished   D exclaimed
    E explained

16 These bolts are much too stiff to loosen by hand. Have you
    got a ....?
    A spanner   B key   C screwdriver   D hammer   E handle

17 This film is not .... for young children.
    A right   B agreeable   C suitable   D adapted   E worthy

18   Grandmother was sitting by the fire, ... a sock.
     A embroidering   B weaving   C manufacturing
     D knotting   E knitting

19   '......... your backs!' shouted the porter, pushing his trolley
     along the crowded platform
     A see   B think of   C pay attention to   D mind   E keep

20   I think we should have .... glass put in the bathroom
     window, Max. The people on the other side of the street
     can see right in.
     A new   B thick   C patterned   D cracked   E frosted

21   Telephone the ...., quick! Water is pouring down the
     stairs!
     A electrician   B plumber   C piper   D engineer
     E builder

22   Run down to the grocer's and get me a bag of flour, Jim.
     I want to .... a cake.
     A boil   B roast   C cook   D toast   E bake

23   She has put .... a lot of weight since last year.
     A on   B in   C down   D up   E off

24   Shall we dance, darling? They are playing our favourite
     ....
     A music   B motive   C tune   D line   E aria

25   Be careful going up the stairs, Grannie. Hold on to the
     ....
     A parapet   B sides   C railings   D edges   E banisters

26   I'm sorry to have to tell you, sir, that this painting is not
     by Rembrandt. It is a clever ....
     A fraud   B artificial   C counterfeit   D fake   E likeness

27   I have never met such .... children as Pamela's. She
     can't do anything with them.
     A funny   B naughty   C evil   D big   E heavy

28 'How would you like your hair cut, sir?' 'Just a ...., please.'
A trim   B snip   C shave   D cut   E tidy

29 Passengers are requested not to use the lavatory while the train is .... at a station.
A running   B standing   C stopping   D entering
E leaving

30 Will you .... some cheese, please, Sally, to put in this sauce?
A chop   B powder   C grind   D grate   E stir

31 He must be terribly strong. Look at his ....!
A skin   B limbs   C hair   D muscles   E nerves

32 This is just a rough .... but it will give you some idea of what the girl looks like.
A sketch   B picture   C design   D plan   E miniature

33 I can't open this case; the .... seems to be stuck.
A lock   B catch   C closing   D bolt   E knob

34 'Do you row?' 'I used to, but I haven't used a pair of .... for years.'
A sticks   B rows   C paddles   D poles   E oars

35 'Will you come to the theatre with me on Saturday?' 'Oh, yes, that will be a great .... for me. I love the theatre but I rarely have the chance to go.'
A experience   B advantage   C opportunity   D treat
E feat

36 Sugar is more expensive now because there was a very poor .... of sugar-beet last year.
A lot   B crop   C harvest   D collection   E gathering

37 I'm sorry I'm late, Mr Grimes. My alarm clock didn't
....
A turn up   B come in   C get on   D go off   E set down

38 The recipe is a secret; it has been .... from father to son
    for generations.
    A made up **B** written out **C** spoken of **D** handed down
    E put off

39 Tomorrow morning the sky will be .... but the sun
    should come out later.
    A covered **B** dark **C** overcast **D** clouded **E** opaque

40 They're very expensive at the new hairdresser's, Edith.
    I had to pay £3 just for a shampoo and ....
    A comb **B** wash **C** set **D** fix **E** stop

Section B

*In this section you will find after each passage a number of
questions or unfinished statements, each with four suggested
ways of finishing it. You must choose the one which you think
fits best. Cross through the letter A, B, C or D for the answer you
choose. Give one answer only to each question. Read each
passage right through before choosing your answers.*

First Passage

We were right on time. Sunshine Tours informed its passengers
on the printed itinerary that their coach was due at the Hotel
Splendido, Rome, at approximately 1800 hours. Glancing at
my watch, I saw that it wanted three minutes to the hour.

'You owe me five hundred lire,' I said to Beppo.   5
The driver grinned. 'We'll see about that in Naples,' he said.
'In Naples I shall present you with a bill for more than two
thousand lire.'

Our bets were continuous throughout the tour. We each kept
a book, checked the kilometers against the time, and then   10
settled up when either of us felt like paying. The latter generally
fell to me, no matter who had come out on top with the betting.
As courier, I received the larger tips.

I turned round, smiling, to my cargo. 'Welcome to Rome,
ladies and gentlemen,' I said, 'the city of popes, emperors, and   15
Christians thrown to the lions, not to mention movie stars.'

A wave of laughter greeted me. Somebody in the back row
cheered. They liked this sort of thing. Any facetious remark
made by the courier helped to establish the relationship between passengers and pilot. Beppo, as driver, may have been   20

responsible for their safety on the road, but I, as guide, manager
and shepherd of souls, held their lives in my hands. A courier
can make or break a tour. Like the conductor of a choir he
must, by force of personality, induce his team to sing in har-
25 mony; subdue the noisy, encourage the timid, conspire with
the young, flatter the old.

I climbed down from my seat, flinging wide the door, and saw
porters and pages hurrying from the swing-doors of the hotel
to meet us. I watched my flock descend, sausages from a
30 machine, fifty all told – no need to count the heads for we had
not stopped between Assisi and Rome – and led the way to the
reception desk.

'Sunshine Tours, Anglo-American Friendship League,' I said.
I shook hands with the reception clerk. We were old acquain-
35 tances. I had been on this particular route for two years now.

'Good trip?' he asked.

'Pretty fair,' I replied, 'apart from the weather. It was snowing
in Florence yesterday.'

'It's still March,' he said. 'What do you expect? You people
40 start your season too soon.'

'Tell them that at the head office in Genoa,' I answered.

Everything was in order. We held block bookings, of course,
and because it was early in the season the management had
fixed my whole party on the second floor. This would please
45 them. Later in the year we should be lucky to get the fifth, and
tucked away in the rear of the building at that.

41 The coach arrived in Rome
   A   at about six o'clock in the evening.
   B   only three minutes late.
   C   earlier than the courier had expected.
   D   later than it usually did.

42 Before arriving in Rome
   A   the courier had borrowed 500 lire from Beppo, the
       driver.
   B   the driver told the courier that he owed him more than
       2,000 lire.
   C   the driver had bet the courier that the coach would
       not arrive on time.
   D   the courier had bet the driver that the coach would
       arrive late.

43   'cargo' (line 14) refers to
    A   luggage.
    B   people.
    C   bets.
    D   tips.

44   Why did the courier want to make the people in the coach
    laugh?
    A   They were bored and tired and he wanted to cheer
        them up.
    B   They were worried about their safety, as Beppo was
        driving.
    C   He hoped that in this way he would get more tips.
    D   He wanted the tourists to feel happy with him as
        courier.

45   According to the writer, a courier must
    A   teach his clients to sing.
    B   have a strong personality.
    C   make or break the success of a tour.
    D   not quarrel with the driver or passengers.

46   Why was it not necessary for him to count the passengers
    as they got off the coach?
    A   It didn't matter how many there were.
    B   He had already counted them in Assisi.
    C   There were 50 seats on the coach and 50 people.
    D   The coach was not going any farther.

47   The tourists on the coach were
    A   English, but friendly towards Americans.
    B   Italians, with English or American relatives.
    C   friends of the courier's.
    D   either English or American.

48   The courier and the hotel receptionist knew each other
    because
    A   the courier always took his tourists to that hotel.
    B   they had worked together two years previously.
    C   the courier had been working on that tour for quite
        a long time.
    D   both the courier and the receptionist belonged to the
        Anglo-American Friendship League.

107

49 The receptionist told the courier that
    A it was too early in the year for that sort of tour.
    B March had been exceptionally cold that year.
    C he should not expect to have snow in Rome.
    D it always snowed in Florence in March.

50 The courier thought that
    A when the tourists came back later on the tour they
       would not have such good accommodation.
    B the tourists who came to Rome later in the year would
       be luckier.
    C they had been very lucky indeed to get rooms all to-
       gether on the second floor.
    D his party of tourists would have preferred to sleep on
       the fifth floor.

Second Passage

No sooner had the door closed behind Miss Parrish than
Crawford picked up the telephone at his elbow and dialled a
number.
    'Reception,' said an impersonal female voice.
5   'This is Crawford,' he said. 'Listen carefully. A woman has
just left my office. She's about thirty-five, tall, with long blonde
hair. She's wearing a blue and white check coat and carrying
a crocodile handbag. Don't let her leave the building.'
    'What shall I tell her, Mr Crawford?'
10 'Use your imagination, Gwen. Make any excuse you like,
but don't let her out of the front door. And for Heaven's sake
don't let her know that I've spoken to you.'
    'All right, but I don't know how long ... Oh, excuse me,
madam, ...' And the receptionist rang off. Crawford realized
15 that Miss Parrish had reached the ground floor. There was no
time to be lost. He dialled another number, and drummed
impatiently on the desk with his fingers as he waited, listening
to the bell buzzing commandingly at the other end of the line.
    'Come on, woman, for God's sake!' he muttered.
20 He let the bell ring for another few seconds, then pressed the
receiver rest down and dialled another number. This time a
voice replied immediately.
    'This is Crawford. Is Simmonds there?'
    'Speaking, Mr Crawford.'
25 'The Parrish woman is here. She's down in reception.'

'O.K. I'll be right over. I'll take care of her.'

'Be careful, Simmonds,' said Crawford, urgently. 'It's got to appear natural. She's got to walk out of here with you of her own free will. There mustn't be anything suspicious about it. There are too many people around down there.'   30

'Don't you worry, Mr Crawford. I've got it all worked out.'

'Good man,' said Crawford. 'Now listen. Be as quick as you can getting here; I don't know how long Gwen will be able to keep her down at the desk before she smells a rat.'

'The car's outside now, Mr Crawford.'   35

'Right. I'll stay here. Call me as soon as you get her to Cavendish House. I've got to talk to Mrs Drake, but she doesn't seem to be at home so I'll have to do some phoning around.'

'She's here, Mr Crawford.'

'What? Mrs Drake? At Cavendish House? What the hell's   40
she doing there?' demanded Crawford in great surprise.

'I don't know. She turned up about ten minutes ago in a great state and said she had to talk to you. I made out that I didn't know where you were and she said she'd wait.'

'Good man,' said Crawford again. 'Can she hear you now?'   45

'No. She's in the drawing-room, drinking brandy as if it was lemonade.'

51 Crawford made his first telephone call
   A as Miss Parrish was leaving his office.
   B immediately Miss Parrish had left his office.
   C before Miss Parrish had left his office.
   D although Miss Parrish had left his office.

52 Why did Crawford describe Miss Parrish to the receptionist?
   A Because the receptionist did not know her.
   B Because Miss Parrish had changed her appearance.
   C Because Crawford wanted to see Miss Parrish.
   D Because the receptionist might have made a mistake.

53 What did Crawford want Gwen to do?
   A Have a long conversation with Miss Parrish.
   B Keep Miss Parrish in the building.
   C Make excuses to Miss Parrish.
   D Make Miss Parrish go out by the back door.

54 Crawford's second telephone call
    A   was to Simmonds.
    B   was answered immediately.
    C   was to Mrs Drake's number.
    D   was to an unknown person.

55 When Crawford made his third telephone call
    A   he did not recognize Simmonds' voice.
    B   he asked if Simmonds was speaking.
    C   he asked where Simmonds was.
    D   he asked Simmonds to speak.

56 Simmonds told Crawford that he would
    A   be very kind to Miss Parrish.
    B   see that Miss Parrish did not run away.
    C   take Miss Parrish to Cavendish House.
    D   kill Miss Parrish.

57 Crawford was afraid that Miss Parrish
    A   might be frightened by the rats.
    B   would attack Gwen, the receptionist.
    C   would try to run away.
    D   might become suspicious.

58 Crawford told Simmonds that
    A   it might be rather difficult to contact Mrs Drake.
    B   Mrs Drake had gone to look for him at Cavendish
        House.
    C   Mrs Drake was not on the telephone.
    D   Mrs Drake refused to speak to him on the telephone.

59 Crawford was very surprised to hear that
    A   Mrs Drake had called him.
    B   Mrs Drake was with Simmonds.
    C   Mrs Drake wanted to speak to him.
    D   Mrs Drake was drinking brandy.

60 Mrs Drake had arrived at Cavendish House
    A   with great formality.
    B   in a very agitated condition.
    C   drunk.
    D   with a lot of servants.

Test Paper 11

Section A

In this section you must choose the word or phrase which best completes each sentence. Cross through the letter A, B, C, D or E for the word or phrase you choose. Give one answer only to each question.

1   I want this roll of film developed and .... please.
    A stamped   **B** made   **C** printed   **D** pictured   **E** finished

2   George is in the garden, cutting .... to burn in the fireplace.
    A forests   **B** twigs   **C** blocks   **D** trunks   **E** logs

3   Linda was wearing a very .... skirt which swirled round her as she danced.
    A tight   **B** loose   **C** big   **D** full   **E** heavy

4   Will you .... this needle for me, please? I can't see very well in this light.
    A fill   **B** load   **C** use   **D** prepare   **E** thread

5   My husband does not feel at all well. I think he must have eaten something that .... with him.
    A disagreed   **B** hurt   **C** disturbed   **D** bothered
    E poisoned

6   Mrs Blenkinsop fell into the swimming-pool with a loud ....
    A crash   **B** splash   **C** rush   **D** whoosh   **E** tinkle

7   I smiled sweetly at her, but she .... at me, so I guessed she didn't want to be friendly.
    A looked   **B** peered   **C** frowned   **D** beamed   **E** grinned

8   These plates are made of a tough plastic material, and will not break or .... easily.
    A drop B crash C shatter D spoil E chip

9   Sign your name on the .... line.
    A drawn B spotted C striped D broken E dotted

10 The plane .... at 6.00 so you must be at the airport by five o'clock.
    A comes out B leaves from C takes off D goes up
    E gets off

11 The lecture was very .... and I slept for most of it.
    A annoying B sleepy C noisy D quiet E boring

12 I am not going to play cards with your brother again. He always tries to ....
    A win B cheat C trick D steal E beat

13 Yes, Amanda can go and play with you in the park, but don't be .... with her.
    A hard B strong C rude D rough E heavy

14 Emily looked very serious in a black dress with white collar and ....
    A hands B bottoms C ends D cuffs E sleeves

15 In the park, dogs must be kept on a ....
    A lead B string C control D cage E chain

16 A fat lady sat on my shopping bag in the bus and .... my tomatoes.
    A squeezed B crushed C broke D squashed E pressed

17 Be careful not to .... the tray too much or the glasses will slide off.
    A throw B bend C incline D twist E tilt

18 I have a sore .... ; perhaps I smoked too many cigarettes yesterday evening.
    A neck B throat C head D chest E mouth

19 You look very different with your hair .... on the right.
    A cut B parted C divided D combed E separated

20   George was wearing a black tie with pink ....
     A points   **B** balls   **C** marks   **D** stains   **E** spots

21   She says she is 45 but her face is so .... that I think she
     must be at least 60.
     A damaged   **B** folded   **C** rough   **D** wrinkled   **E** creased

22   May I please have a glass of water? I feel a little ....
     A ill   **B** hungry   **C** bad   **D** ache   **E** faint

23   I have a .... on my leg where you hit me.
     A wound   **B** hole   **C** bruise   **D** blister   **E** spot

24   Aunt Edna has never married; she is a ....
     A maid   **B** spinster   **C** bachelor   **D** single   **E** virgin

25   Martin .... several photographs at our party.
     A made   **B** had   **C** got   **D** took   **E** shot

26   I want some roses with nice long ...., please.
     A stems   **B** legs   **C** trunks   **D** branches   **E** feet

27   Carla was wearing a black leather belt with a big silver
     ....
     A button   **B** buckle   **C** fastener   **D** link   **E** knob

28   Be careful what you say to Martha. She is rather ....
     these days.
     A quick   **B** sore   **C** angry   **D** sensible   **E** touchy

29   We shall have to have the deck-chairs repaired. The
     canvas has ....
     A broken   **B** torn   **C** burst   **D** split   **E** cracked

30   I missed the last three lessons because I was ill; now I am
     working hard to ....
     A catch up   **B** get on   **C** make way   **D** come to
     E find out

31   I have been looking at this letter for half an hour, but I
     still can't .... the signature.
     A write down   **B** see to   **C** watch over   **D** make out
     E find out

32 Peter picked up a .... and went out to clear the snow
   away from the front of the garage.
   A shovel B hammer C fork D sword E rake

33 The train had to stop because there were several cows on
   the ....
   A platform B rail C tunnel D route E line

34 Look at all those holes in my winter coat! I am afraid the
   .... have been at it.
   A worms B butterflies C birds D moths E insects

35 A child suddenly ran out into the street and I had to ....
   to avoid him.
   A stop B deviate C swerve D turn E skid

36 The .... is a teaspoonful, to be taken three times a day.
   You must not exceed it.
   A measure B quantity C remedy D medicine E dose

37 May I go and wash? I have been eating honey and my
   fingers are ....
   A sweet B sticky C wet D dirty E yellow

38 There was a sudden thunder-storm, and, as we had no
   raincoats, we got wet ....
   A completely B quite C altogether D over
   E through

39 That fish smells terrible! Throw it in the ....!
   A rubbish B waste-paper basket C sink D dustbin
   E refuse

40 When I was invited to a .... -dress party last month,
   I went as Adam and I wore a large fig-leaf.
   A funny B special C historical D masquerade
   E fancy

Section B

*In this section you will find after each passage a number of
questions or unfinished statements, each with four suggested*

ways of finishing it. You must choose the one which you think fits best. Cross through the letter A, B, C or D for the answer you choose. Give one answer only to each question. Read each passage through before choosing your answers.

First Passage

It was still dark when I awoke and the terrace outside was almost white in the moonlight. I knew that it was a sound that had awakened me, but I did not know what sound. I looked across at Rosalie asleep on the other bed; but she was quite still. There was a small table between the two beds and I could   5
see the dial of my watch glowing there. It was three forty-five.

Just then I heard the sound again. It came from away along the terrace. A man said something sharply and there was a noise like a packing-case being moved on concrete.

I swung my legs to the floor and stood up. My bath-towel was   10
lying between the beds and I wrapped it around my waist. If I were going to have to tackle an intruder, I preferred not to do so stark naked.

I bent over Rosalie and kissed her. She stirred in her sleep. I kissed her again and she opened her eyes. I kept my head close   15
to hers.

'Wake up, but speak softly.'

'What is it?' She was still half asleep.

'Listen. There's somebody trying to get along the terrace from one of the empty apartments. Thieves, I suppose. I'm   20
going to scare them away.'

She sat up. 'Have you got a revolver?'

'Yes, but I hope I won't have to use it. They're making a lot of noise. They probably think there's no one here.'

My suitcase was under the bed. I got the revolver out,   25
rotated the cylinder until one of the three rounds in it would fire when I pressed the trigger, and went over to the window.

There was a wall separating this section of the terrace from that belonging to the unfinished apartment next door, and it had iron spikes on it. I heard one of the men cursing as he tried   30
to negotiate them. Now was the moment to act, I thought. As I had told Rosalie, all I wanted to do was to scare them away. If either of them got down from the wall, he would be cornered with nowhere to run.

I stepped out on to the terrace.   35

41 Why did the writer wake up?
  A He did not know why.
  B Some men made a noise in the street.
  C There was too much noise for him to sleep.
  D Someone next door made a noise.

42 How did he know what the time was?
  A The bedroom was not completely dark.
  B He switched on the bedside lamp.
  C His watch had a luminous face.
  D He could hear his watch ticking.

43 . . . someone was moving a packing-case on concrete.
  A He was afraid that
  B He was angry because
  C It sounded as if
  D A man's voice told him that

44 Why did he wrap his bath-towel round his waist?
  A Because he wanted to have a fight.
  B In order not to shock Rosalie.
  C Because he had been sleeping naked.
  D Because he would not be able to tackle an intruder
     without one.

45 He woke Rosalie very gently because
  A she would have been frightened.
  B he did not want her to make a noise.
  C he was afraid that they would be attacked.
  D he wanted her to help him scare the thieves away.

46 The writer thought that the thieves were making a noise
  because
  A they didn't realize that he and Rosalie were in that
     apartment.
  B they were trying to move packing-cases around.
  C they wanted to frighten him and Rosalie.
  D they didn't want him to attack them.

47 He took his revolver out of his suitcase and
  A loaded it.

B fired it.
C turned it round.
D prepared it.

48 Why were there iron spikes on the wall?
  A To keep intruders out of the apartment.
  B To stop people going from one terrace to another.
  C To separate the two adjoining apartments.
  D To hurt possible intruders.

49 Why was one of the men cursing?
  A Because his negotiations were very difficult.
  B Because he realized that the writer had heard him.
  C Because he didn't know the writer could hear him.
  D Because it was not easy to climb over the spikes.

50 The writer wanted to
  A frighten the man before he reached the terrace.
  B corner the man so that he would not be able to escape.
  C make the man run away into a corner.
  D scare the man when he got down from the wall.

Second Passage

Mrs Henderson was not happy about the flight – not happy at all. It wasn't that she hadn't flown much before; in fact, she thought of herself as quite a hardened traveller, going as she did every summer to visit one of her numerous relatives in various parts of the world. She was on her own; her job was   5 well-paid, and she lived quite modestly for the greater part of the year, so that when holiday time came around she was able to undertake quite spectacular journeys. Why, only last summer she had flown out to visit her younger daughter in Auckland, and had returned by way of Japan and the States,   10 and in all those many hours of flying she had not felt the slightest discomfort. In fact, she had thoroughly enjoyed it.

Why, then, this nagging fear about such a short journey? After all, Amsterdam is only a stone's throw from London in terms of air travel. She had done the trip before, several times.   15 No sooner are you up and your seat-belt undone than you have to fasten it again for the landing at Schiphol.

'Good morning, Madam,' said the pretty hostess, with a flashing smile, as Mrs Henderson arrived, a trifle breathless,

117

20   at the top of the entrance stairs. 'May I see your boarding-card, please? 25 F. Yes, that's right at the back of the aircraft, on the left, just by the emergency door.'

      'Thank you,' murmured Mrs Henderson. She knew perfectly well that the seat was next to the emergency door. She had
25 chosen it for that express reason, although she could not have said why she wanted to be in that particular seat on this particular flight, when such fancies had never troubled her in the past.

      As she carefully folded her tweed coat and tried to fit it
30 neatly into the minute cupboard that was provided for the purpose above her seat (she decided that her hat, small though it was, had better stay on her head), a phrase rang through her head.

      'Second sight, that's what she has. Second sight, they call it.'
35 It had been a family joke, some twenty-five years before. Their next-door neighbour at that time, a somewhat simple-minded woman by the name of Nellie Parsons, had asked Mrs Henderson (young, newly-wed Mrs Henderson as she was then) to help her choose a holiday hotel. Mrs Henderson had told
40 her that she didn't think the Hotel Majestic (which Nellie had already tentatively decided upon as it was marginally cheaper than the others) looked very good, and said that if she were going to Braydon for her holiday she would rather stay at the Hotel Bella Vista. Nellie was only too glad to have her mind
45 made up for her, and had a most enjoyable holiday with her children at the Hotel Bella Vista, marred only by the fact that during their stay there was a disastrous fire at the Hotel Majestic, and six people were killed.

      When she came back to Downton Avenue, she was lavish in
50 her praise of Mrs Henderson's prophetic powers.

      'Just think! We might all have been burned to death in our beds. What an escape! Second sight, that's what she has. Second sight, they call it.'

      And it was useless for Mrs Henderson to protest that she
55 had simply thought that the Hotel Bella Vista, on the strength of its brochure, looked more comfortable. She and Henry had often laughed about Nellie's claim that she had second sight. But why should it have come into her head just now?

51 Mrs Henderson
    A was used to flying.

B flew everywhere.

C didn't like flying.

D flew away every summer.

52 How was Mrs Henderson able to afford to make such long holiday journeys?

A She was a very rich woman.

B She had no husband or young children.

C She saved up her money between holidays.

D She only stayed with members of her own family.

53 Why was Mrs Henderson going to Amsterdam?

A To visit a relative.

B For a short holiday.

C Because she was afraid.

D We don't know why.

54 The air-hostess asked to see Mrs Henderson's boarding-card

A to discover whether she had a ticket or not.

B to find out where she wanted to go.

C to see where she was going to sit.

D to know who she was.

55 Why had Mrs Henderson chosen seat 25 F?

A She always liked to be near the emergency door.

B She never flew in any other seat.

C Because there was a cupboard above it.

D She did not know why.

56 Did Mrs Henderson take her hat off?

A Yes, and put it in the cupboard with her coat.

B No, she put it on before she sat down.

C No, there was no room for it in the cupboard.

D Yes, it was too small for her and uncomfortable.

57 Nellie Parsons

A had already decided to spend her holiday at Braydon and asked Mrs Henderson's advice about hotels.

B didn't know where to go for her holiday and asked Mrs Henderson to give her some advice.

C didn't want to stay at the Hotel Bella Vista because it was very expensive.

D asked Mrs Henderson which hotel she had stayed at when she went to Braydon.

58 Did Nellie Parsons follow Mrs Henderson's advice?
A Yes, but rather reluctantly.
B No, she went to the Hotel Majestic.
C Yes, and very willingly.
D No, because the Hotel Majestic was cheaper.

59 Nellie Parsons claimed that Mrs Henderson
A was able to foretell the future.
B was a most valuable friend.
C was able to see everything twice.
D had advised her to go to the Hotel Majestic.

60 Mrs Henderson did not understand why
A she had unexpectedly remembered a remark made many years before.
B Nellie Parsons had claimed that she had second sight.
C she and her husband had laughed about what Nellie Parsons had said.
D Nellie Parsons would not believe that she didn't have second sight.

Test Paper 12

Section A

In this section you must choose the word or phrase which best completes each sentence. Cross through the letter A, B, C, D or E for the word or phrase you choose. Give one answer only to each question.

1   Do you .... Mrs Shepherd's telephone number?
    A remind **B** recall **C** think **D** remember
    E call to mind

2   Agnes was .... with fear. 'I daren't go home now,' she whispered.
    A quivering **B** shuddering **C** trembling **D** moving
    E throbbing

3   The house was built more than a hundred years ago. My father had it .... when he bought it.
    A renewed **B** altered **C** changed **D** transformed
    E conformed

4   The tap kept .... all night long, and I could not sleep.
    A dropping **B** pouring **C** dripping **D** rushing
    E leaking

5   '......... your feet before you come into the house,' called Aunt May.
    A clean **B** rub **C** wash **D** wipe **E** polish

6   Don't leave your coat lying on the chair like that, Frank. Hang it up by the .... at the back of the collar.
    A hole **B** hook **C** thread **D** loop **E** band

7   They returned by a different ....
    A trip **B** excursion **C** direction **D** route **E** map

8 Look at this beautiful bag! I only paid £4 for it at Harridges' sale! It was a real ....
A affair B occasion C cheap D bargain E benefit

9 It hasn't rained for weeks, but the grass was quite wet with .... early this morning.
A water B shower C frost D dew E drops

10 I had no idea she was such a liar. She .... me completely.
A deluded B deceived C disappointed D deprived
E pulled

11 As he ran, the coins and keys .... in his pocket.
A clanked B rustled C rang D clattered E jingled

12 Two, four, six, eight and ten are .... numbers.
A pair B dual C even D right E double

13 A .... of £500 is offered for information leading to the arrest of the robbers.
A prize B fee C award D tip E reward

14 I think I need a holiday; I have been feeling rather ....
lately.
A downcast B below standard C off colour
D under strength E out of mind

15 .... the tube gently, so as not to waste the toothpaste.
A press B hit C squash D squeeze E twist

16 His trousers were so tight that when he bent down suddenly they .... with a loud noise.
A fell B opened C tore D split E broke

17 I don't believe a word of that story! You are pulling my ....
A leg B nose C hair D teeth E ears

18 Luckily, the pistol was not .... so nobody was hurt.
A loaded B charged C full D stocked E ready

19 It's quite a long story, but, to put it in a ...., Mr Jones
    has been dismissed.
    A phrase B nutshell C teacup D thimble E sentence

20 Take this ...., Henry, and fetch some water from the
    stream so that we can all have a wash.
    A cup B bucket C sack D kettle E spoon

21 After I had failed my driving test for the sixth time, I lost
    .... and decided not to try again.
    A faith B heart C conviction D stomach
    E encouragement

22 These oranges are full of ....
    A pips B seeds C stones D nuts E grounds

23 That was a stupid ...., Bill, to pull Aunt Rose's chair
    away just as she was going to sit down.
    A action B fun C movement D joke E trick

24 A box of matches, a pound of tomatoes, a loaf of bread and
    a small .... of chocolate, please.
    A bit B piece C log D bar E stick

25 The police believe that the man they are looking for may
    be .... as an old blind beggar.
    A dressed B acting C disguised D pretending
    E seeming

26 I'm afraid this stain on your jacket just won't ...., sir.
    A go away B die down C move off D come out
    E make off

27 She put her hand up to her eyes to shade them from the
    .... of the oncoming lights.
    A light B shine C stare D power E glare

28 There's an ambulance just behind us, Paul, and it's in a
    hurry. Pull over on to the .... and let it pass.
    A verge B border C centre D edge E road

29   The advantage of this new plastic covering is that it will
     .... to fit any size of object.
     A expand B grow C stretch D extend E change

30   I don't think I know that song, Madam, but if you can
     .... the tune I may be able to recognize it.
     A call B chant C sing D mouth E hum

31   Ines was wearing a pure white dress, with a gold belt
     round her ....
     A knees B hips C neck D bust E waist

32   'Can you .... something for the hospital?' she asked,
     rattling a collecting-box under my nose.
     A give B provide C leave D spare E save

33   'Can you tell me the way to the station, please?' 'Yes, go
     straight down that street. Just follow your ....'
     A legs B eyes C nose D sight E line

34   When they saw the police car turn the corner, they dropped
     the sticks they were holding, took to their .... and fled.
     A legs B feet C toes D heels E wings

35   Come on, Betty, ... yourself together. There's nothing
     to cry about.
     A bring B hold C keep D pull E take

36   I can't .... wondering why Uncle Simon hasn't written
     to us since his last visit.
     A go B help C quite D prevent E bear

37   Mr and Mrs Price .... their silver wedding last week.
     A had B celebrated C congratulated D made
     E marked

38   Nobody has seen Anna since she left home last Monday
     morning. She seems to have .... into thin air.
     A vanished B dissolved C changed D become
     E gone

124

39 How many marks did you .... for that algebra home-
    work you did last night?
    A get **B** make **C** take **D** score **E** become

40 We hold a meeting every two weeks; on every ....
    Thursday evening, in fact.
    A both **B** odd **C** other **D** following **E** alternative

Section B

*In this section you will find after each passage a number of
questions or unfinished statements, each with four suggested
ways of finishing it. You must choose the one which you think
fits best. Cross through the letter A, B, C or D for the answer you
choose. Give one answer only to each question. Read each passage
right through before choosing your answers.*

First Passage

*The writer is at a luncheon-party in the home of Edward Driffield,
a very old and famous writer.*

The duchess joining in the conversation at the head of the
table, the vicar's wife turned to me.
    'You knew him many years ago, didn't you?' she asked me in
a low tone.
    'Yes.'   5
    She gave the company a glance to see that no one was
attending to us.
    'His wife is anxious that you shouldn't call up old memories
that might be painful to him. He's very frail, you know, and the
least thing upsets him.'   10
    'I'll be very careful.'
    'The way she looks after him is simply wonderful. Her
devotion is a lesson to all of us. She realizes what a precious
charge it is. Her unselfishness is beyond words.' She lowered
her voice a little more. 'Of course, he's a very old man, and old   15
men sometimes are a little trying; I've never seen her out of
patience. In her way she's just as wonderful as he is.'
    These were the sort of remarks to which it was difficult to
find a reply, but I felt that one was expected of me.
    'Considering everything, I think he looks very well,' I   20
murmured.
    'He owes it all to her.'

125

At the end of luncheon we went back into the drawing-room, and after we had been standing about for two or three minutes
25 Edward Driffield joined me. I was talking with the vicar, and for want of anything better to say was admiring the charming view.

'I was just saying how picturesque that little row of cottages is down there.'

30 'From here.' Driffield looked at their broken outline and an ironic smile curled his thin lips. 'I was born in one of them. Strange, isn't it?'

But Mrs Driffield came up to us. Her voice was brisk and melodious.

35 'Oh, Edward, I'm sure the Duchess would like to see your writing-room. She has to go almost immediately.'

'I'm so sorry, but I must catch the three-eighteen from Tercanbury,' said the duchess.

We filed into Driffield's study. It was a large room on the
40 other side of the house, looking out on the same view as the dining-room, with a bow window. It was the sort of room that a devoted wife would evidently arrange for her literary husband. It was scrupulously tidy and large bowls of flowers gave it a feminine touch.

45 'This is the desk at which he's written all his later works,' said Mrs Driffield, closing a book that was open face downwards on it. 'It's a period piece.'

We all admired the writing-table, and Lady Hobmarsh, when she thought no one was looking, ran her fingers along its under
50 edge to see if it was genuine.

41 Why did the vicar's wife speak to the writer in a low voice?
    A   She did not want their conversation to be overheard.
    B   She wanted to tell him something private and personal.
    C   The Duchess might have been listening to what they said.
    D   What she wanted to tell him was a very important secret.

42 Mrs Driffield was anxious that
    A   her husband should not remember the past.
    B   the writer should not speak to her husband.
    C   her husband should not be upset in any way.
    D   no one should hear the vicar's wife's remarks.

43 The vicar's wife told the writer that
   A Mr Driffield was rather a difficult old man.
   B Mrs Driffield's work was hard but she didn't complain.
   C Mr Driffield was very lucky to have such a devoted wife.
   D old men sometimes do not try very hard.

44 Although it was difficult, the writer replied to the vicar's wife's remarks because
   A he agreed with what she had said.
   B · she had asked him several questions.
   C she was waiting for him to say something.
   D it would have been very rude to have said nothing.

45 'He owes it all to her' (line 22). 'It' in this sentence refers to
   A Driffield's reputation as a writer.
   B Mrs Driffield's devotion to her husband.
   C Driffield's state of health.
   D the Driffields' wealth and social position.

46 Why was the writer admiring the view?
   A Because he thought it charming and picturesque.
   B In order to get into conversation with Driffield.
   C Because he was talking to the vicar at the time.
   D He had nothing else to talk about at the moment.

47 When Driffield says 'From here' (line 30) he means that
   A the row of cottages was a long way from his house.
   B the cottages were really more picturesque than they appeared.
   C the row of cottages looked better from a distance.
   D he had moved from one of the cottages to his present house.

48 Why did Mrs Driffield interrupt their conversation?
   A She wanted Driffield to take the Duchess to the writing-room.
   B She didn't want her husband to start talking about the past.
   C She didn't want the Duchess to know that he was born in a cottage.
   D Because the Duchess was ready to leave for Tercanbury.

49 What was the writer's impression of Driffield's writing-room?

   A Driffield had written all his best books there.
   B It was too big and tidy to be comfortable as a writing-room.
   C It had a good view of the cottages where Driffield was born.
   D It seemed to reflect Mrs Driffield's personality more than her husband's.

50 Lady Hobmarsh thought that
   A the writing-table was too beautiful to be true.
   B Mrs Driffield was not telling the truth.
   C nobody had been paying attention to her.
   D the writing-table might not be a real antique.

Second Passage

Emily saw the mirror when she examined the objects for sale in the Balring Auction Rooms in New York. It was an old mirror, dirty and stained, in a red lacquered frame. She wanted the mirror the moment that she saw it, but she walked quickly
5   away from it, reconciled to the fact that she would never have it.
   Her seat was the one that she had always occupied when her mother was alive, seventh row centre and on the aisle. Emily watched the people come in. She did not know any of them, although she recognized many of them as auction regulars.
10 She thought about the mirror. She would not bid for it, of course. She had never bid for anything. Neither had her mother.
   Emily's mother had liked to watch people. She was interested in what they bought at an auction and in how much they paid.
15 She could talk happily about the objects and the bids for the rest of the week until it was time to go to another auction. Emily had listened and had interjected appropriate comments but she had never been that interested in auctions. She was mildly interested in this one but only because of the mirror.
20 The auction was a slow one, and Emily wondered what the people who bought stuff planned to do with it. The gavel* fell for the last time and the mirror had not been offered. Emily walked over to it, nearly colliding with Mr Balring.

*gavel (a small hammer used by auctioneers when selling by auction)

He said: 'Good evening.' That is all he had ever said to her.
She had never said anything to him. She had to brace herself 25
now.

'Mr Balring!' He turned. 'You did not auction the mirror.'

'The mirror?'

'Yes, the one with the red lacquer frame.'

'Oh!' He seemed startled. 'That! No. I guess not. Do you 30
want it?'

'How much are you asking?'

'Twenty dollars.'

Emily retreated within herself and Mr Balring saw the
retreat. 35

'You are an old customer of mine, aren't you? You and
.........?'

'My mother. She has been dead for four months. We never
missed one of your auctions, not since the first we attended
eight years ago. We weren't exactly customers.' Emily heard 40
her voice go on and on, appalled at herself. She was not normally
a talker.

Mr Balring took a backward step. 'An old customer,' he
repeated, 'a valued customer. I'll let you have the mirror for
ten dollars.' 45

'I'll take it.'

Emily spoke before she thought. She did not need the mirror,
but Mr Balring had turned away from her to speak to a man
who was sitting behind a table, writing in a large account book.
The man rose and walked slowly towards her. 50

'You bought the mirror?' he said. 'Ten dollars?'

'Yes. Mr Balring wanted more. He made a special price for
me.'

51 When Emily first saw the mirror
    A she decided that she would like to buy it.
    B she did not look at it very carefully.
    C she thought that it was not for sale.
    D she realized that she could not buy it.

52 Why did Emily go to the Auction Rooms on that day?
    A She wanted to buy a mirror.
    B She liked watching people at auction sales.
    C She went from force of habit.
    D She had nothing else to do that day.

53 Many of the people who came to the auction
    A   were known to Emily by sight.
    B   were professional antique dealers.
    C   always attended Balring's auctions.
    D   greeted Emily as they entered the rooms.

54 Although Emily and her mother had attended auction
    sales regularly
    A   they had never been able to afford to buy anything.
    B   they were too nervous and shy to bid for anything.
    C   they had never made any attempt to buy anything.
    D   nobody in the rooms knew who they were.

55 Emily's mother had liked going to auction sales because
    A   she bought a lot of useful things there.
    B   she was fascinated by old furniture.
    C   she was interested in other people's behaviour.
    D   she liked the friendly atmosphere that she found there.

56 Emily went to the auction sales with her mother
    A   because she had nothing else to do.
    B   because the old lady liked her to go.
    C   although she was not specially interested.
    D   because her mother could not have gone alone.

57 The mirror was not sold during the auction because
    A   nobody made an offer for it.
    B   it was too dirty and old-fashioned.
    C   the auctioneer did not try to sell it.
    D   nobody had wanted to pay 20 dollars for it.

58 Emily
    A   wanted to talk to Mr Balring.
    B   found it difficult to speak to Mr Balring.
    C   and Mr Balring did not usually speak to each other.
    D   would have liked to speak to Mr Balring.

59 Emily was 'appalled at herself' because
    A   her mother had only been dead for four months.
    B   she was talking in a very foolish way.
    C   Mr Balring thought she was talking too much.
    D   she did not usually behave in that way.

60 Emily bought the mirror
    A because Mr Balring had reduced the price.
    B because she was an old and valued customer.
    C without really intending to do so.
    D quickly, before Mr Balring could change his mind.

Place figures of a future . . .
B. because we starting out ? place of the prop—
B. Decisions we say you'll tell us about our goals
C. culture we be explained in a
D. make a judgment . . . of the read of true . . . mind